D0305651

TREES & DEER

How to Cope with Deer in Forest,
Field and Garden

RICHARD PRIOR

TREES & DEER

How to Cope with Deer in Forest,
Field and Garden

Drawings by Jeppe Edrup

SWAN·HILL
PRESS

Copyright © 1983 and 1994 by Richard Prior

This edition first published in the UK in 1994
by Swan Hill Press, an imprint of Airlife Publishing Ltd.
Presiously published in 1983 by B.T. Batsford Ltd.

British Library Cataloguing in Publication Data
  A catalogue record for this book
  is available from the British Library.

ISBN 1 85310 432 9

Printed by Butler and Tanner Ltd., England.

Swan Hill Press
an imprint of Airlife Publishing Ltd.

101 Longden Road, Shrewsbury SY3 9EB, England.

Contents

Acknowledgements

This book is produced in association with the British Deer Society. I am extremely grateful to the Society's Patron, H.R.H. The Prince of Wales, for honouring the book with his Foreword. Their President, Lord Dulverton, has been a source of constant encouragement and inspiration.

No thanks are sufficient for the friendly and generous way that stalkers, foresters and scientists have shared their knowledge over the years. Not least my collaborators in assembling the information, Jeppe Edrup, whose lively drawings need no additional commendation, and Judy Pittock, who kept me and endless scribbled sheets in order with unfailing patience and tact.

Particular acknowledgement should be made for the help of present and past colleagues in the Game Conservancy and Forestry Commission. Also to these long-suffering readers for their constructive and informative comments: from the British Deer Society, Lord Dulverton C.B.E., T.D., M.A., D.L., Dr A. McDiarmid D.Sc., PhD., M.R.C.V.S., F.R.C. Path, F.R.S.E., Walter Buckingham, Arthur Cadman, Peter Davenport and John Hotchkis (law); from the Forestry Commission, Roger Larsen, Barry Teasdale and Andrew Neustein; from Deer Management Consultants, Kenneth Macarthur O.B.E., Ole Daugard Petersen and Captain Andrew Wills; also Dr Helmuth Strandgaard, Game Biology Station, Kalo; Professor Reino Hofmann, Geissen University; Ronnie Rose, Economic Forestry Group; Louis Petyt, Federation of E.E.C. Hunting Organisations (F.A.C.E.).

I would also like to thank the following individuals and organisations for permission to reproduce their photographs:
Raymond E. Chaplin   1, 4
Ian McCall   12
John Marchington   7
Game Conservancy   13, 14, 15
Forestry Commission   2, 3, 5, 8, 9, 10, 11, 13, 14, 15

ST. JAMES'S PALACE

From the copses of southern England to the vast northern conifer plantations, our woods and forests are a great national asset. We need them for much-needed timber production. We need them at the same time to beautify the landscape, to provide quiet enjoyment and recreation and, not least, to harbour as wide a variety of wildlife species as possible.

Deer are the largest and perhaps the most beautiful of our land mammals, but they do eat trees - to the despair of forester and gardener alike. Achieving harmony between managers of land and the wildlife it supports is vitally important.

We must learn to plan and plant in ways which will avoid damage, or at least not invite it. Equally, deer must be controlled humanely and effectively, for their own health as much as for crop protection. A higher degree of understanding and mutual help must be built up between forester and deer stalker.

This book opens up new ground in the management of deer with the needs of forestry clearly in mind. Speaking as a former President of the Royal Forestry Society and Patron of the British Deer Society, I have found Richard Prior's experience and forward - thinking advice of great value. Today we are suffering from the results of a planting policy devised some 50 years ago, which took little account of wildlife management and paid scant attention to any consideration other than straightforward timber production. But, learning from these lessons, we now have an opportunity to be more imaginative in terms of forest design, landscaping, recreation and wildlife management. Richard Prior's contribution in this area is most timely and much to be welcomed. I am sure this book will interest all those concerned with the future of British woodlands and wildlife.

Introduction

Richard Prior's knowledge of and experience among deer make this book indispensible both to 'deer men' and to foresters who have problems with deer.

The wide open spaces of the Highland hill country, where the traditional red deer 'forests' lie, are being ever increasingly planted up with trees, and although the natural habitat of the wild red deer was the vast natural forest of earlier days, these new, much needed forests often deprive the deer of the kinder areas of ground, on which they depend so much in the harsh Highland winters. The new forests of the twentieth century are protected by 6ft high deer fences, but the deer in their battle for survival generally force or find their way in and inflict damage – often grave – on the growing trees.

Not only in the Highlands, but throughout Britain, from John o'Groats to Dorset, other species of deer – roe, fallow, and the exotic sika and muntjac – are increasing and spreading their range. They, too, cause problems, not only to foresters, but also to farmers and gardeners.

There are really two phenomena here, which are comparatively new in Britain, and of course they are inter-related. One is the great increase in forestry; the other, partly as a result of this, an increase in the wild and feral deer populations.

We foresters, farmers, gardeners, naturalists, sportsmen, and those of all categories who value these most intriguing and beautiful of our national fauna – need to learn new methods of controlling deer populations, not only to prevent the damage that they can cause, but in their own interests too.

The author of this book has so wide an experience of deer, their habits and means of humane control, from the high tops of the Scottish deer 'forests' to the woodlands of southern England, that I cannot recommend too highly the contribution which it makes to the knowledge and progress of enlightened and efficient deer management in Britain.

Lord Dulverton, President: British Deer Society
President: Timber Growers Scotland

Section 1

Forestry and Deer Damage

1 *Deer Damage: The Basic Facts*

Attitudes to deer tend to fall into two camps: The Bambi Syndrome – the impression that every time a deer dies there is one less of these lovely creatures in the world – and the Wild West approach; 'The only good deer is a dead deer!'. Urban opinion, fostered by Walt Disney and the like inclines towards the first. Foresters, because of their sufferings at the hands of these fascinating but infuriating animals, have a good deal of sympathy with the second.

The sad fact is that deer eat trees; some species eat little else. They are also a very successful group of mammals in an era when many forms of wildlife are threatened by the pressures of civilisation. The population of truly wild deer in Great Britain probably exceeds one million, of six different species. At least 300,000 'bambis' are born every year, to live out their life-span on a diet of trees and bushes, grass and corn, market garden crops and suburban roses. By definition, a similar number die. We have eliminated the bears, wolves, lynxes and other predators which absorb the annual surplus in more primitive countries. If we do nothing to limit numbers by sensible and humane culling, the job will be done with grim efficiency by starvation and disease, natural controls which the most ardent of the Bambi faction would shrink from experiencing in real life. In addition, these controls would not operate before we had suffered an unacceptable level of damage to farm and forest crops.

Conservation has been defined as the wise use of a renewable resource. The conservationist's answer to the continued existence of deer in this country is that a reasonable compromise can be found between deer on the one hand and forestry and farming on the other, so that the cash return balances the damage and costs involved. In this way both can exist without major conflict.

The forester has to suffer from the attentions of deer to the extent that serious costs are incurred, but he is at the same time under pressure, either from his own affection for deer and other wildlife, or from public opinion, to make sacrifices in their favour, and allow them to live in his woods. The limit of any sacrifice, whether in terms of loss of plantable ground or the percentage of damage considered to be tolerable, and the various concessions to be made are a basic management decision upon which the tactics of subsequent actions have to be based. Nor will this necessarily remain static from one year to another. The aims and priorities must also be critically examined. In the majority of cases these will almost certainly be:

1   Keep forest damage to an acceptable level
2   Maintain a healthy deer herd within the
natural carrying capacity of the area
3   Balance the inevitable costs involved by
marketing a reasonable annual deer harvest

The latter may be in terms of venison, live sales, utilising deer by-products such as antlers, skins etc., or additionally by letting the sport of stalking, provided this is done under proper safeguards. The presence of deer can also be turned into a recreational asset, for example by letting high seats for photography or deer watching (*see* Chapter 11), or enclosing representative specimens in a park in connection with other public attractions.

In order to achieve a reasonable balance between forestry and deer, understanding is needed of the reasons for damage, and of ways to avoid it,

so that we neither invite the deer to do unnecessary harm, nor create conditions in the woods which make deer control needlessly difficult and time-consuming.

When deer eat trees the action is known as *browsing*. In addition they rub their antlers up and down the stem, thus destroying the bark – *fraying* – and on occasions they take the bark in their teeth and pull it off, presumably to satisfy some physiological need. This action is called *bark stripping* or *peeling*. Seeing his trees killed or stunted, or exposed to disease with the costs of establishment raised accordingly, any woodland manager is likely to react violently against the perpetrators. Yet this is only akin to a police murder hunt which may catch the murderer, but can do nothing to restore the victim to life; once a tree is damaged, the harm has been done. No matter how important action might be when more young trees are likely to suffer damage, prevention should have anticipated and forestalled much of the trouble. *Most of the problems suffered by forest owners from deer could have been avoided at the planning stage of the plantation.*

Clearly, the existence of deer, and the number which are able to get at the trees while at a vulnerable age, has a direct bearing on damage. If density is excessive and the deer are short of natural food, heavy damage is inevitable. The stalker's part is to control numbers. Trees may, however, be planted or treated in such a way that even a small population of deer can be highly destructive. Equally, a plantation may be laid out so that the stalker cannot see or control the deer except by chance. It cannot be emphasised too strongly that the best time to avoid damage is before the trees are planted.

Much unnecessary conflict arises where deer stalking and other sporting rights are divorced from forest management. In this case, when concessions have to be made by the forestry side to permit deer shooting, for example by

leaving space unplanted, the forester is likely to feel aggrieved because of the sacrifice of plantable land, even if he will benefit in the long run. Deer, and pheasant shooting for that matter, have a definite annual value (*see* Chapter 12) and if reckoned in terms of discounted revenue as a part of the forest product, can make a very substantial contribution to it.

The smaller the scale of planting, the easier it is for the deer to lie up in safety in or near to the vulnerable crop and, therefore, the worse the damage is likely to be. To quote a south country example, Cranborne Chase in Dorset used to be an area of coppice-with-standards where the hazel was traditionally worked by hurdle-makers. As this industry declined, various trials were made during the early post-war years in conversion to high forest. The surviving hurdle makers would obligingly clear a small patch, perhaps quarter to half a hectare, which was planted up to a beech-conifer mixture, producing a chequer-board effect. About the same time a neighbouring owner was striving to achieve a two-tier forest by thinning the canopy of existing conifer plantations and underplanting shade-bearing species in small groups. In both these cases the damage by roe deer was dramatic.[1]

Another experiment was prompted by the bare floor which develops under hazel. Trees were planted without opening up the canopy, where the deer ate them in seclusion and complete safety. Nine years later those that survived were still much the same size, not only because of the attentions of the deer, but for lack of light. Like many other forestry experiments, this technique was not allowed time to demonstrate its failure before thousands of acres were treated in the same way, with similarly bad results. It was called the 'Dark Ages Planting' among those involved.

If these misfortunes were frustrating to the foresters, they provided a stimulating workshop in which to study the causes of damage. Not least because of the varying degrees of success displayed in adjoining forests, where similar problems were tackled in different ways. The most damage was caused, and the least could be done about it from the point of view of control, where sufficient cover was left in the plantation for the deer to feel safe. Deer of all species also have an uncanny instinct to find and demolish anything out of the ordinary. Exotic tree species, whether hardwood or conifer, must always be regarded as especially vulnerable. Semi-standards put in for ornament or landscape effect will be singled out for attack, while orchards, nurseries and gardens are likely to be raided, and need special precautions.

The bigger deer species, red, fallow and sika, have a preference for grazing rather than browsing, if equally attractive alternatives exist. In fact, most problems with the latter two species are concerned with agricultural rather than forest damage, although neither of them are entirely blameless. All three can prove a first-class pest when tender agricultural crops are planted close to woodland. Some of the damage done is particularly annoying, for example the habit they have of taking one bite from a root vegetable, probably pulling it out of the ground and leaving it to rot, while the deer goes on to the next in line. Such promiscuous ruination of a crop, and nightly visits to young grass or corn by large numbers of deer have to be countered one way or another. A few animals out in a field should not automatically be assumed to be doing material damage, especially if the deer in the area are being managed, and are making their own contribution to the estate finances in return for their keep.

In the north, red deer exist in large numbers and under harsh conditions. Their periodic incursions from the hills, whether into farmland or forest, are grievous for the managers of either to bear. Although the management of hill red deer is outside the compass of this book, we are concerned with them as invaders of planted land, and with the inevitable colonists which, having returned to the forest, their natural environment, decide to live and breed there.

An estimate has been made that 400,000 hectares of new planting in Scotland has been made in or adjoining land normally inhabited by red deer. Many miles of deer fencing have been erected to exclude them, at enormous cost. This has given rise to a form of Parkinsonism: The capital cost of fencing has been authorised, but only at the expense of the labour needed to patrol and maintain the fence, once erected. Professor Mutch of Edinburgh University has claimed that a deer fence is unlikely to be effective for more than 15 years, and the majority of fenced plantations will have been penetrated by red deer (not to mention roe) within 12 years. A heavy snowfall can make any fence ineffective in one hour.[2]

In the period following the Second World War, a vast area in the north of England and Scotland has been planted for the first time since the disappearance of our primaeval forests. Usually with the aid of deer fencing in red deer country these new forests are now growing up, to the satisfaction of investors and foresters, and to the eventual profit of the nation. We have benefited from the fact that open ground was being enclosed. This advantage will never recur as stands of timber come to maturity and are harvested, to be replanted for the second rotation. Aided by windthrow, an uneven-aged forest will result, inhabited by deer all too willing to emerge from their thickets to ravage any new planting.

Deer control, therefore, cannot be relaxed immediately the first rotation is established, nor must our forests be laid out, as many unfortunately have been, with a total disregard of the needs of the deer stalker. Merely erecting a fence is no long-term answer, but its effectiveness can be vastly increased if it does not, for example, cut across traditional migration routes, or totally enclose deer wintering grounds so that the deer are forced to break in, or perish starving against the fence.

Once inside, deer are likely to gorge themselves with unaccustomed plenty, but some at least will soon try to escape. Further attempts will be made when the midges are bad in July, and towards the rut, as far as the red deer are concerned. Practically every deer-fenced enclosure in Scotland has a black tramped path round the inside. Finding themselves trapped, the stags fray to relieve their frustration, and considerable damage can be done. Eventually the deer become hefted to the plantation, and afterwards have to be treated as truly woodland deer, not as interlopers.

Provided they are properly managed, these woodland red deer, with roe and other species if they are present, are capable of living in this environment without causing undue damage in the context of extensive forestry. In contrast, the perpetual harrassment to which they are subject in certain areas of Scotland night and day, in season and out, often has adverse effects; the costs are formidable because the deer become extremely shy; in addition, deer subject to constant disturbance never settle to a natural feeding timetable, and damage, particularly by peeling, can be intensified. It has been shown that deer under such stress are unable to accumulate necessary fat reserves in the late summer, leading to emaciation and exaggerated forest damage during the winter.

To summarise, the presence of deer in an area makes some impact on forestry and farming inevitable. Information on the species and advice on their habits is essential and understanding the root causes of damage is the key to positive, balanced action. Much can be anticipated and avoided by forethought and planning, some can be minimised even after planting. Deer control obviously has a vital part to play in reducing density to the minimum practical level, and thereafter managing the population efficiently to make its own contribution to the forest product. If the stalker is to do this, he needs the active collaboration of everyone involved. Protection strategy can be divided into three categories:

1   Forestry options:
       planning operations
2   Control:
       density
       population structure
3   Stalker efficiency:
       training
       management
       equipment

Information on the biology of the various deer species, with the exception of muntjac, is now more readily available. Woodland stalking technique is also better understood, and courses are run by the British Deer Society and the Game Conservancy, and by the Forestry Commission for their own ranger staff. How to apply this relatively new knowledge to the prevention of damage is examined in the following chapters.

2 *Damage Investigation and Assessment*

If damage is reported, identify the species responsible, assess the percentage of trees affected, the significance to the plantation, when the damage was done and whether it is likely to recur.

Prompt reporting, accurate information, and objective appraisal are the keys to effective action in the event of damage occurring. All too often the time for correcting the trouble has long passed by the time it is noticed, frequently with the result that general retribution is demanded. This is not likely to be effective. Another feature of damage reports is the likelihood that the original report (which is possibly inaccurate to begin with) becomes distorted and exaggerated as it passes from one person to another along the chain of management.

Damage Identification

Any casual report of damage is usually attributed to deer to avoid responsibility and blame. Because it is likely to be more severe near any paths or rides, and through an unconscious desire to give weight to the incident, the extent and serious nature of the outbreak tends to be inflated. Before taking action the woodland manager is well advised to go and see for himself. A quick tour round by Land Rover is not sufficient. The plantation needs to be carefully walked to see how large an area is affected and whether, and to what extent, the damage is concentrated, or scattered throughout the crop. Quite unexpected hazards may be revealed through this.

The Forestry Commission has developed a damage assessment technique based on random sample plots in large plantations which is helpful in avoiding a subjective judgement which may not be confirmed by the facts. The problem with this method is that the degree to which damage is scattered throughout the crop is fundamental to its significance. Methodical sampling does however reveal the extent of different causes of tree loss, and gives a factual basis for assessing the importance of deer damage as one facet of the problem.

Physical or climatic conditions must then be considered and eliminated (or otherwise) as a cause of plant losses. Trees are unfortunately subject to many disasters especially in the first few years. Drought may kill. Bad planting technique is often to blame, while poor, dried-out plants may never root properly. Pulling up one or two casualties will soon reveal this cause of death. Frost can kill or check, and trees checked by frost may resemble very closely others checked by browsing. If trees on slightly higher ground appear to be more successful, a regular frost pocket can be suspected, or alternatively faulty drainage. Unfortunate choice or timing of chemical

Part damaged	Appearance of damage	Season	Type of damage	Evidence		Species responsible
				Width of toothmark	Height above ground	
Stem or trunk	Bark stripped in well defined pieces. Toothmarks parallel and more or less vertical	Dormant	Winter bark stripping	8–9mm	0.3–1.7m	Red
				4–5mm	0.5–0.6m	Roe
					<1m	Fallow/Sika
	Bark stripped in small pieces. Toothmarks parallel and oblique. Often on lower branches and stem	Dormant	Bark nibbling	2.5mm	<0.5m	Rabbit
				3mm	0.6m	Hare
				<1.3mm	0.15m	Voles
		Mostly Mar–June	Bark nibbling		any	Squirrel
	Bark stripped in vertical bands	Active	Summer stripping	Evidence of species present – slots, droppings		Deer
					Height	
	Bark torn off in strips often on one side. Few or no broken side branches. Wood underneath scored	1 Feb–20 May	Fraying (velvet)		<0.80m	Roe
		15 July–15 Sep			<1.80m	Red
		1 July–31 Aug			<1.60m	Fallow/Sika
	Bark torn off in strips, often all round stem, side branches twisted and broken	1 Apr–15 Aug	Fraying (territory)		<0.80m	Roe
		15 Sep–31 Oct	Fraying (velvet and rut)		<1.80m	Red
		15 Sep–31 Oct			<1.60m	Fallow
					0.17–0.5m	Muntjac
		Mar–Apr	Spring fraying		<1.80m	Red
					<1.60m	Fallow

Damage	Type	Timing	Plant state	Measurement / Indication	Species
Stems prodded into holes (mostly conifers)	Fraying (Rut)	Nov–Dec		Stems <12mm	Chinese Water deer
	Fraying (Rut)	Sept–Nov		Stems <10cm / 15–38cm	Sika
Buds and twigs eaten – cut ends rough with chewed appearance	Winter browsing	Dormant		Maximum height of damage: 1.50m Red; 1.40m Fallow; 1.15m Roe; 56–86cm *Muntjac	
Buds or twigs	Summer browsing (mostly hardwoods)		Active	Height-species as winter + indication of species i.e. tracks, droppings, hair.	Deer
Buds and twigs eaten. Cut ends a clean oblique sheared appearance	Winter browsing	Dormant		Width of incisor / Height of damage: 2.5mm / <0.50m Rabbit; 3mm / <0.70m **Hare + indications of species i.e. tracks, droppings, holes	Rabbit / **Hare
Buds or ends of shoots picked off	Leaf flush	Early spring		On young plants <.60m + indication of species i.e. tracks, droppings, feathers	Capercaillie or Blackcock

Note:
* Muntjac frequently browse to the second height by standing on their hind legs
** Bitten twig often lying on the ground below

treatment can also check trees. Reference to compartment history records can be revealing.

Having eliminated death or checking from these causes, or taking them into consideration for a proportion of the total lost, evidence of insect or fungal pests should be searched for; then, signs of small mammals and birds. Voles flourish in grass mat, and their holes will be seen everywhere. Damage by field voles (*Microtus agrestis*) is usually at the root collar, but bank voles (*Clethrionomys glareolus*) are agile climbers and bark may be removed at any height, resembling peeling or fraying damage by deer, unless the twigs are examined carefully. Foliage may also be found if their tunnels are opened up.

Much damage is, of course, done by rabbits and hares. Fortunately these rodents make a clean diagonal bite so that the twig looks as if it had been pruned with a pair of secateurs. Particularly in the case of hares, the cut piece will usually be on the ground nearby. In contrast, deer-browsed twigs show a rough end, often partly cut by the lower incisors (deer have no upper incisors) and pulled off, leaving a tongue of bark. Otherwise they put the whole frond into their mouths and chew it off with the molars. Equally, the cut has a ragged end. Clean, diagonal cuts of more than 45 degrees usually denote an error by the weeding gang – sometimes jocularly referred to as 'Sheffield Blight'. Rabbits and hares also chew bark, especially in snow. Later, once the snow has melted, this damage may be misleading because of the distance from the ground. Making allowance for this fact, the height of the browse line can give a good indication of what animal is responsible.

When examining an established crop, by stooping down it will be possible to see that most or all greenery has been removed up to a certain height if pressure on the trees is at all severe.

	Max. height (approx.)
Rabbits	<0.5m (1ft 8in)
*Muntjac	0.56m–0.86m (1ft 10in–2ft 10in)
Roe	1.20m (4ft)
Fallow or sika	1.40m (4ft 6in)
Red deer	1.50m (5ft)

* Muntjac frequently browse to the second height by standing on their hind legs

Cattle, sheep and goats are also keen browsing animals, capable of doing serious damage if left to themselves. In judging what has been eating the trees, great care should be taken to eliminate the possibility that domestic stock is to blame.

While a theory has been formulated that a sheep-bitten twig can be distinguished from one chewed by deer because the ragged tongue arises from the centre in the case of sheep, and otherwise from the side, one would need to be very experienced to be really sure. Fortunately there is an easier method: sheep's wool is extremely durable, and a brief search along the fence will soon supply plenty of evidence if they have been in. Cattle are often driven through the woods from one field to another, browsing as they go. The evidence they leave behind is no less specific if you fail to look where you are going. Goats are notorious for their appetite for leading shoots, leaves and twigs. Domesticated goats have been known to escape, so damage in the vicinity of a farm with goats must be suspect. Feral goats are now found in a number of areas, particularly in Scotland. In hard weather they are very likely to descend from the hills in search of food and shelter. In these places an effort must be made to separate the damage done respectively by goats and deer. Their droppings and footmarks should be studied.

Where fraying is noted, the height at which bark has been removed is indicative of the deer species responsible:

Muntjac	<0.50m (1ft 8in)
Roe	<0.80m (2ft 7in)
Fallow or sika	<1.60m (5ft 3in)
Red	<1.80m (5ft 11in)

Roe deer choose relatively clean stems on which to fray, but red and fallow deer with their greater strength often break off or shred a number of small side branches. Roe choose trees or bushes which fit conveniently between the buck's antlers, and thin enough to flex when he exerts his strength. Thus, it is possible to some extent to work out who the culprit is. A heavy adult buck with wide spreading antlers may choose a tree from 2.5cm to 8cm (1in to 3in) or more in diameter, which would be far too resilient for a yearling. Roe fraying stocks will have a triangular scrape at the base of the tree. Young territorial bucks dig at these scrapes more assiduously than older bucks whose status is assured. Damage to ride-side trees can also be done by tractors and other vehicles, and this possibility should be borne in mind.

Damage Assessment

In assessing the liability of damage to recur, allowance should be made for exceptional circumstances, such as unusually heavy snowfall, breach of the fence by a falling tree, or sudden influx due to forestry operations in neighbouring blocks. Once the leading shoot is above normal browsing height, clipping of the side branches has much less significance. Because of this, plantations are vulnerable to roe deer browsing for a comparatively short time, especially if there is no extended period of beating-up. Fraying continues until the stems are too large or the side branches too strong. Larch is the principal sufferer, and if the need to cut down challenges to territorial roebucks has not been dealt with by a heavy cull of yearlings, damage can be serious from this cause for some years after the leaders are out of reach.

Clearly, every effort must be made in the early years of a plantation not only to avoid or reduce damage, but also to get the trees off to as good a start as can be managed so that the vulnerable period is as short as possible. If, through adverse soil or drainage conditions, too much competition or poor planting technique, they get a bad start in life, extra years are added to this expensive and frustrating time.

In poor upland areas the application of fertiliser, usually ground rock phosphate, will benefit the young trees and help them to get a good start. However, it will also make the trees and herbage beneath them more attractive to the deer. In such cases the provision of alternative food supplies is vital. Ride treatment to give a short sward sweetened with periodic applications of nitrogen and lime may well be justified by reducing pressure on the trees. Scrub for browsing, either left for the deer or deliberately planted, should also be encouraged.

3 *Minimising Damage*

The time to forestall deer damage is before the trees are planted: before the land is cleared, fenced or ploughed. The way each of these operations is carried out can be the keystone of future success in establishing the new crop and can determine the efficiency and ease of deer control operations throughout the next rotation. The liability of each plantation to deer damage should be assessed as part of normal planning in exactly the same way as the need for drainage or any other physical feature of the site. If a bog is to be planted, the possibilities of lowering the water table are discussed, calling in a specialist for advice if necessary. Nobody plants the trees first and then worries about drainage when they are all dead. The presence of deer is no less a hazard to successful forestry, but similar forethought in planning to prevent trouble is a real rarity.

Naturally, some methods of coping with deer in plantations are necessarily direct, but may not be as successful or as cost-effective as might be assumed. Attempting to kill all the deer in the wood, or fencing them out completely are actions which come within this category. Other possibilities may be capable of producing good results, either to complement direct action or as alternatives.

The philosophy of damage avoidance can be summed up in this aphorism:

Don't fight nature –
Encourage it to go away!

That is to suggest that the forester, from his knowledge and understanding of deer, does nothing which will unnecessarily increase the damage they do. Curiously, there is much in common between the management of deer and the management of people. We now recognise, from our knowledge of human behaviour patterns, that to protect an area by erecting 'Trespassers will be Prosecuted' signs is likely to provoke vandalism. Small direction signs, however, indicating some feature in the opposite direction are likely to be followed. Even the leisured holiday-maker has two basic fears in woodland; fear of getting lost and fear of wasting time (or, putting it another way, of failing to see something about which he may be asked later). Thus knowledge of human natural history is utilised to avoid damage. Deer behaviour can be used in the same way, and often with spectacular results.

Planning

In all the multitude of things to decide upon and arrange before a piece of ground, no matter how small, can be planted, who can be surprised if future problems concerned with deer filter to the bottom of the pile? Weather conditions, ploughing, plant supplies, labour, grants, transport – all must be coped with, usually in a rush, but to what end if the trees so carefully planted are eaten the same night, or worse, in five years' time? In the case of open ground afforestation the ability to visualise the landscape when the trees have grown enough to hide the deer is half the battle in anticipating and frustrating problems which will arrive at that stage.

Information is needed on the species and numbers of deer, not only on the land to be planted but also in the vicinity. Seasonal movements may be anticipated, for example in the event of bad weather. These could create additional pressure on vulnerable crops. Red deer are not alone in shifting their ground, fallow deer have been observed to move up and down hill according to changes in temperature. Some fallow herds also wander apparently at random in a fairly large home range, possibly five or six miles across. Some of this is in response to disturbance or the location of attractive crops. In the autumn they accumulate at traditional rutting stands which may be thinly populated at other times. Later, disturbance due to pheasant shooting may initiate other significant movement. Even roe deer, though normally static as adults, may desert some woodland in the winter. In parts of the north, woods are used to over-winter stock which makes them completely inhospitable to deer until new ground cover appears the following spring. New plantations in hill country may be too cold through the winter months, but hold a full stock of roe for the rest of the year. In this case the colonists tend to be surplus juveniles from nearby, and fraying damage can be serious in consequence. Neighbouring ground may carry very heavy deer stocks in the winter. Damage can therefore be out of proportion to the deer density in summer.

Fraying

Fraying causes the most obvious damage, partly because much of it affects ride-side trees and those just inside fenced plantations. The sight of peeled stems is infuriating and it is easy to jump to the conclusion that conditions are equally bad throughout. Fraying for the removal of velvet, which takes place from March to May with roe, and in late summer for the larger species, is usually absorbed by a few scattered trees. Roe, being territorial, then use the same trees and others about their territories to act as visual and olfactory

markers. As well as warning off incursive bucks by the sight of these fraying stocks, secretions from their foreheads are used as a scent signal. Well established territorial bucks have enough authority and presence to dominate youngsters by barking and threat demonstrations. They also appear to establish a tacit understanding with their neighbours over territorial boundaries which avoids the need for repeated confrontations. In contrast, young non-territorial roe bucks have to assert their vitality and aggression by constant demonstrations of fraying. This takes place when challenging an established buck for his territory as well as between bucks of the same age class. If a group of such youngsters settles in a plantation the damage can be serious.

Red stags in fenced plantations can create havoc if unable to escape. Otherwise fraying by red and fallow is likely to be very localised. Fallow deer have traditional rutting stands which, if planted up, will almost certainly be ravaged by the bucks. These stands are small. In Wyre Forest near Kidderminster, for example, old charcoal burning hearths are favoured. These areas, if left unplanted and incorporated into a design for future deer control, will produce an annual crop of deer over the next rotation. If planted and beaten-up year after year the expense will be totally unjustified. If planted and left, the deer damage is unlikely to produce a usable control clearing. During the rut, red and fallow fraying is mostly confined to the immediate vicinity of their rutting stands rather than being scattered as in the case of roe. One unfortunate feature of roe fraying habits is their predilection for anything unusual. A few flowering or exotic trees planted for ornament are sure to be attacked. Arboreta deserve special protection in consequence.

For some unexplained reason, fallow bucks and red stags resume fraying for a short period in the spring, just before the antler cast. Mock fights also happen at this time. Apart from special cases such as these, fraying can be controlled to a level where it is unlikely to be economically significant,

though disfiguring, to a plantation. Provided the reasons for it are understood, measures can be taken to avoid creating conditions where serious damage is unavoidable.

Fraying damage by roe deer can be tackled in four ways:

1   Cut competition by young bucks
2   Ensure a reasonably level sex ratio
3   Protect especially vulnerable or non-commercial trees
4   Provide alternative scrub to absorb fraying pressure

Cutting competition

A heavy cull of surplus yearling bucks early in the season, preferably before they start to fray, will have a dramatic effect on the amount of fraying damage. No matter what the aims of management may be – the reduction of damage, the production of venison, or building up trophy quality – harvesting a proportion of the annual production immediately after the period of maximum weight gain, and before damage commences, is good management practice. They will soon be thrown out by the adults and probably lost to the estate that nourished them.

Some woods, because they are unsuitable for territorial adults, will act as receiving areas, surplus yearlings accumulating there in quite large numbers. In such places a very heavy cull may be called for, plus an appraisal for the reasons for this influx. It is better to have a couple of resident bucks than many contentious youngsters. Removal of one territorial buck early in the season may lead to a group of yearlings taking his place.

Level sex ratio

The connection between fraying damage and the need for equal numbers of bucks and does may not be immediately clear. Reproductive success and overall deer density are dealt with in following sections. However, another element has to be considered: If the doe cull is neglected in favour of pleasant and sometimes profitable buck stalking, a surplus doe finding herself without a consort at the time of the rut will go and search for one *and bring him back to her home range.* The bucks thus seduced, often from considerable distances, will probably be juveniles. The management plan is thus demolished, and damage increases once more.

Protecting vulnerable or ornamental trees
Individual protection or various forms of fencing may be justified when damage is inevitable even if the local deer population is reduced to a minimum or where special considerations apply. This is more fully explored in Chapter 4.

Alternative scrub for fraying
Assuming that total elimination of the deer in a newly planted area is impossible or undesirable, some fraying will have to be accepted. Whether this is serious or not depends primarily on the degree that the crop is affected. If all natural scrub is destroyed, for example by the use of herbicides before planting, nothing remains for the deer to use for fraying other than valuable trees. Some species, like larch, are attractive to roe as fraying stocks but others will be left alone if a scattering of scrub is left for the deer to use. Bill McAvish, then Chief Forester at Kielder, was the first to demonstrate the advantage of planting willow at intervals through a spruce plantation for this purpose. With a bundle of willow sticks under his arm as he walked behind the planting gang, he would thrust one in every hundred yards or so. A year or two later most of the willows had taken, and every one had been attacked by roe while the crop was largely untouched. This idea has been developed over the last 20 years and is covered in more detail in Chapter 7.

Just as willow, ash, rowan and so on can be planted specifically to attract the attention of deer in places where they are likely to come, the converse is equally true: if attractive species are planted in places where deer can get at them, damage is inevitable, unless they are effectively protected immediately they are planted. Tomorrow morning is likely to be too late!

Bark Stripping (Peeling)
The reasons why deer eat bark have been the subject of much research. The habit is mainly confined to red, sika and fallow deer, although roe have been reported to be responsible for localised damage in southern Scotland on lodgepole pine. Starving deer will, of course, eat anything, but otherwise bark seems to represent a physiological need in response to some deficiency. In deer parks, established trees may escape attention for years but then suddenly the bark is stripped and considerable damage can be done. In Melbury Park in Dorset horse chestnut trees were attacked in this way in the spring of 1980. There was no obvious cause or change in conditions in the park to account for the outbreak.

Some of the worst examples of stripping have been reported from the Continent in forests where red deer are fed hay and concentrates. In the vicinity of the feeding places a very high proportion of the trees, mainly Norway spruce, are completely ringed. One assumes that this artificial food needs to be balanced by fibre, represented by bark. The deer are not hungry enough to range far from the feeding stations but content themselves by stripping the surrounding trees.

Another serious cause of peeling damage is disturbance. Deer, being ruminants, like to feed, rest and chew the cud on a fairly short time-scale.[3] By preference, feeding takes place at intervals throughout the daylight hours as well as at night. Red, fallow and sika are grazing rather than browsing animals and find much of their food in the fields and in the grassy woodland glades. Human disturbance interrupts their feeding rhythm and keeps them, hungry and under some stress, in the plantations.

The effect, in terms of peeling damage, of changed conditions is clearly demonstrated at Rold Skov in Denmark. In the 1970s a law was passed giving the public free access to all woodland over ten hectares. Rold Skov is a large forested area in private ownership where red and roe deer existed in reasonable harmony with productive forestry. The whole area was fenced and, prior to the change in the law, closed to the general public. Soon it was noticed that the feeding habits of the deer had changed, red deer no longer being seen out feeding during the day as they were disturbed by ramblers. At the same time, a dramatic outbreak of peeling commenced, remarkable not only for its severity but for the fact that all the damage was on the same side of the tree, clearly done by deer as they faced outwards toward the ride and the source of danger. Brashing exposed the stems of the trees to this type of damage and the only solution offered at the time was the use of the bark plane on selected stems. This tool in effect wounds the tree slightly at intervals up the bole, causing resin to weep out and secure the bark more strongly. This is an expensive operation and the forester remarked that it was easy to do as much damage as the deer if the plane is not carefully adjusted and used. There was, however, no question as to its effectiveness. Most of the trouble was confined to Norway spruce although sitka, with its tougher bark, had also been affected to some extent.

Fallow deer are responsible for some peeling, mostly on hardwoods in the loafing areas where they spend many of their idle hours. Ash and willow are the species most commonly affected. One serious case of damage to 15 to 20-year-old beech was almost certainly due to a change in farming policy: the damage coincided with the arrival of a large sheep flock. Sheep are anathema to all deer and this fallow herd forsook their accustomed fields and were forced to spend most of their time in the woods.

Sika have so far proved to be the least troublesome deer in the forest in contrast to agriculture, where they can be a problem. Apart from one serious and unexplained case of peeling damage to sitka spruce near Peebles, the only real damage to forest crops which is regularly reported is the habit of some sika stags in the New Forest of prodding large fir trees with their antlers until they literally make holes in them. Serious outbreaks of forest damage have, however, been reported from other countries. As sika are extending their range, especially in Scotland, they may become more of a problem.[4]

There is a widespread idea among stalkers that bark stripping is a habit which is catching, and that if the originator is found and eliminated, the trouble will go away. Maybe this is true in certain cases, but the underlying reason for one individual taking bark is likely to affect the rest of the herd, or at least other animals of the same sex.

Tree species with bark which peels easily are more likely to be attacked.

For example Norway spruce is more vulnerable than sitka spruce, lodgepole pine than Scots pine. Bennetsen suggests that greater spacing at planting, a radical thinning before the canopy closes, and early removal of internal deer fences have the effect of distributing the deer more widely, and of reducing the damage by up to 50 per cent.[5]

Bark stripping by domestic stock, particularly on hedgerow hardwoods, is commonplace. What triggers it off in the areas where stock and tree have long term association is still conjecture.

Browsing

Browsing damage by red deer is probably the most serious problem, followed closely by that of roe, though their smaller size means that the vulnerable period after planting is correspondingly shorter. Fallow and sika will also browse but under normal conditions severe damage only occurs where there is either over-population or a local concentration. Higher altitude plantings suffer more than low ground due to climatic conditions restricting the food supply.

Measures to avoid trouble have to be planned before the trees are planted. They have, of course, to be within the constraints of silviculture; even so, the forester often has the choice of options, for example, between two tree species, one of which may be less attractive to deer than the other.

Both long- and short-term requirements to avoid damage should be examined at the planning stage. For example, wide rides for extraction and deer control, needed at the thicket stage and later, may seem to involve a needless waste of plantable land when everything is bare. Widening may, however, prove to be impossible at first thinning because of the risk of windblow.

Half a million acres (201,000 hectares) of open ground in Scotland were planted up in the eight years prior to 1980. In nearly every one of these new forests no provision whatever has been made to enable the deer to be controlled once the deer fence has been penetrated. Colonisation by red and roe deer is inevitable at any time from the present day to the end of the century. *The consequences of this lack of forethought will be suffered by foresters for a hundred years.*

Forward planning to avoid damage by browsing should be tackled in two ways:

1   By thoughtful forestry technique and lay-out

2   By efficient deer control

Methods of deer control will be considered at a later stage. The forestry aspects of damage avoidance can be divided as follows:

Size and shape of plantations: edge effect

Cover – overhead and nearby

Hot-spots

Weeding techniques

Alternative species

Timing

Size and shape: edge effect

The most extreme cases of the effect of size on the amount of damage to be expected can be seen, on the one hand, in moorland afforestation where, apart from the incursions of red deer, the whole forest is unlikely to hold deer until the majority of the plantations are established. At the other end of the scale is the technique of group under-planting in vogue during the 1960s, which allowed deer free and safe access to the new trees. Damage was not only inevitable and serious – or catastrophic – but control in such thick cover was difficult or impossible. This compares with the relative ease of spying and shooting deer on the wide open spaces while the plantations are still lower than the shoulder of a deer.

Woodland deer of all species are secretive, evading danger from man by the use of cover rather than by escape, as is the case with hill deer, red or roe. Similarly they use their ears rather than relying on sight. In consequence, the further a woodland deer is from cover, the more apprehensive he becomes. The amount of time spent feeding decreases as his distance from safety lengthens. Damage is most intense in a narrow band next to thicket or other cover. If the total area of a plantation is large this narrow band of browsing may not be significant: If, because the clearing is small or long and narrow, then a 10- or 15-yard band round the perimeter could represent a major percentage of the whole. Damage, therefore, is proportionately less in plantations which are large and square, where the perimeter is less in proportion to the total area. The less holding cover there is on this perimeter, naturally, the better. If the situation dictates that small areas, or long narrow ones, have to be planted up, then damage is to be expected and precautions must be taken.

Cover – overhead and nearby

Making the deer feel uncomfortable, exposed to danger, is the foundation stone for reducing browsing damage. Removal of all cover before planting makes for a cold, dangerous, unattractive place for deer. Equally, if adjacent areas used by them for warm and safe lairs during the day can be cleaned out of ground cover, so much the better. Often this involves brashing, an operation which lets the wind into a plantation sufficiently for the deer to move out. The further they have to travel from cover to feed, the less damage will be suffered there. Brashing is unfashionable nowadays. A limited amount may well be justified if it protects the latest planting.

Hot-spots

Any stalker knows certain places which are favoured by the deer. Often the banks of a stream are a sure find, maybe a sunny bank or gulley. These are 'hot-spots' and pose a problem to the forester if they are planted up. The deer seem determined to eat anything that is planted there, regardless of species. Left unplanted, such places are invaluable to the stalker. He can be pretty sure of regular success, especially in the difficult business of getting enough does. Practical considerations of money wasted beating-up against regular returns of venison dictate that such places should remain open, part of the small sacrifice of potentially plantable ground which has to be made in the interests of effective forest management.

Weeding

Hand weeding, perhaps the hardest and most disagreeable of the woodman's tasks, is declining because of the cost. From the point of view of preventing deer damage nothing could be more welcome. A sure recipe for disaster is for a gang of men to advance down the rows cutting everything from around each tree. This operation leaves, in effect, a deer path with edible produce (the young trees) proffered at intervals down it while at least some of their alternative browse has been destroyed. Cover left between the rows is likely to hide the deer and give them a feeling of safety.

Even before the development of chemical and mechanical weeding techniques, some foresters managed to limit browsing, and fraying in addition, by reducing the degree of weeding as soon as the growth of the plants would permit. By doing no more than freeing their tops, the plants soon became encased in a matrix of bramble and coppice growth which effectively prevented the deer from getting at them. In addition, there was an abundant supply of preferred browse.

Chemical weeding, if it takes the form of spot treatment around each plant, does not make paths from tree to tree, although each one is somewhat exposed. Treatment of whole lines on the other hand can be nearly as bad as full hand weeding. The Forester at Etal in Northumberland demonstrated an experiment he had done in a plantation subject to heavy browsing. When applying a herbicide he had applied it down the lines over half the area, and between the lines for the rest. One method exposed the trees, while the other reduced weed competition but left some down the line of plants, partially protecting them. Eighteen months later the difference in browsing between protected and unprotected trees was remarkable.

Another chemical application has less happy results. This is the treatment of standing hazel coppice with herbicide immediately prior to planting. The cover remains, slowly dying, but still sheltering the deer while all browse apart from the young planted trees has been eliminated. At a later stage the hazel falls over, the dying against the dead, creating a lattice-work through which no bullet can penetrate, even if the deer could be seen at all.

Mechanical weeding, because the machine works between the rows, leaves a protective screen round each plant. Row widths are usually slightly wider to allow this, which makes the deer easier to see. Occasionally the tractor driver is instructed to take his machine first down, and then across, the lines. Unless the spacing is very wide this nullifies the protection the trees get from one pass along the rows, although it does make deer more visible to the stalker, for instance, within range of a high seat.

Alternative species

Although the choice of tree species is largely determined by physical considerations, (soil, climate, exposure, and so on) and by current economic trends, the forester usually has some latitude. Where deer damage is likely to affect the costs of establishment, he can choose the least susceptible species from among his options – Scots pine rather than lodgepole pine for example, or sitka spruce instead of Norway spruce.

The ideal would be to have a preference table for all tree and shrub species. Sadly, conditions vary too much. In general, transplants are taken in preference to naturally-grown saplings. Anything which is odd or unusual will be singled out, whether it is one spruce in an oak wood, or one oak in a spruce wood. Outside trees and those along rides will also get more than their fair share.

There are, however, some trees which are particularly attractive, even among the species which are grown extensively: red oak (*Quercus rubra*), for example, among the hardwoods; all the willows, and many poplars. Lodgepole pine (*P. contorta*) stands out as a particularly succulent conifer; Lawson's cypress is also high on the list; larches, though less palatable, are very vulnerable to fraying by roe, even several years after planting.

A few species are recognised as low on the list of preferences: Corsican pine (*P. nigra*) is often left alone. Szukiel states that in Poland the grey alder (*A. incana*) is also resistant to deer browsing.[6] For those who attempt to establish a ground layer of cover for the benefit of game, two low-growing shrubs may be grown without protection. Snowberry (*Symphoricarpos rivularis*) flourishes on alkaline soil, to the extent that it can get out of control. Shallon (*Gaultheria shallon*) produces low cover in acid conditions. Deer hardly ever touch either species. In *The Ecology of Red Deer* by Mitchell, Staines and Welch,[7] the following table of research findings is given.

Ranking Orders of Browse Preferences by Red Deer.
(The data of Dzięciolowski (1970c) was obtained by 'cafeteria' trials on one male calf.)

Author	Area	Highly preferred	Preferred	Seldom or never browsed
Sablina (1959)	White Russia	*Salix* *Populus tremula* *Fraxinus* *Quercus*	*Sorbus aucuparia* *Betula*	*Tilia* *Carpinus*
Dzięciotowski (1970c)	Poland	*Quercus petraea* *Salix caprea* *Sorbus aucuparia* *Corylus*	*Acer platanoides* *Carpinus* *Prunus serotina* *Frangula alnus*	*Pinus sylvestris* *Juniperus*
Bobek, Weiner & Zieliński (1972)*	Poland	*Populus tremula* *Salix caprea* *Frangula alnus*	*Quercus robur*	*Tilia cordata* *Carpinus* *Betula*
Ueckermann (1960)	West Germany	*Populus tremula* *Quercus borealis* *Abies* *Acer platanoides* *Fraxinus* *Quercus*	*Pinus sylvestris* *Picea abies* *Fagus* *Pseudotsuga* *Larix*	*Picea sitchensis* *Alnus* *Betula*
Ahlén (1965a)	S. Sweden	*Fraxinus* *Salix* *Frangula Alnus*	*Betula*	*Alnus*
Chard (1966)	NW. England	*Juniperus* *Quercus borealis* *Pinus contorta* *Picea abies*	*Larix* *Acer pseudo-platanus* *Pinus sylvestris* *Quercus* *Betula*	*Picea sitchensis* *Fagus sylvatica* *Alnus glutinosa*

*Includes roe deer browsing

Timing

Pursuing the idea of planting with the minimum proximity to deer-holding thicket, one way of minimising the risk of serious damage is to choose a year when the adjoining plantations have become bare underneath, or when they have just been brashed, or thinned, making them unattractive to deer.

One often comes across forestry plans which involve progressive replanting to be spread over several years. Equally, the sheer size of modern open-ground, large-scale afforestation schemes means that planting the entire area is a long-term operation. Purely from the point of view of avoiding damage, consideration should be given to the practicability of progressing in one direction so that each year's planting is adjacent to the last which, even though growing well, one hopes will not be high enough to hold deer until the adjacent planting is well away. Plans were made recently to plant 400 acres of open land in southern England over a ten-year period. Originally the idea was to plant for the first five years in successive blocks but then go back and add a second block in year six adjacent to the first year's plantation, and so on. Clearly this would have put the later years at unnecessary risk, as each new block would suffer from the attentions of deer already resident in the five-year-old trees adjoining. Because the scheme was discussed with a wildlife advisor at an early stage, it was agreed that each year's block would adjoin the last, so that thicket and valuable trees were never near enough to create a hazard.

Similarly, one arm of a large block of hazel coppice was replanted with Douglas fir (a species susceptible to damage) over three years. By complete clearance, leaving no cover, and by taking each section in succession, the replanting was achieved without noticeable damage even though the population of roe and fallow was very high.

Another question of timing affects certain species, notably oak. All the oaks are very attractive to deer. If browsing is experienced it may sometimes be endured for a couple of years while the plants grow a good root system, even though they may resemble gooseberry bushes. Then the main stem can be cleanly cut with a hook to allow a strong leader to develop. One or two years' undamaged growth should be enough to see the leader above the browsing height for roe (1.1m [3ft 6in]). Naturally the plantation needs to have an unusual degree of protection during this comparatively short time; either electric or other temporary fencing, individual guards, or the ruthless attention of a stalker during the vulnerable period. In the latter case his efforts should be reinforced by the use of deterrents.

4 *Protection*

Fencing is essential for large-scale afforestation schemes in red deer country. Equally, physical protection of some sort is needed for ornamental or small-scale planting where deer of any species are present. Where the purpose of the plantation is strictly commercial, some damage is probably tolerable, and protection measures can be balanced against increased cost of establishment, e.g. investment in fencing compared to the cost of one or two years' extra weeding, possibly plus beating up.

Information on the proportion of damage really attributable to deer is difficult to assess accurately, but at least a careful and objective survey as described in Chapter 2 must be carried out. However, if additional costs are involved, *and the scale of planting is large enough*, then full-scale fencing may be justified. The graph on the following page shows how quickly the length of fence and therefore the cost per hectare is reduced as the size of enclosure approaches 50 hectare (120 acres).[8] Even so, the capital outlay is enormous, and if the forest has been laid out originally to make deer control possible, such costly measures should rarely be necessary.

With the thought for the long future which is a hallmark of forestry, today's foresters should be alive to the needs of their successors when planning new areas for planting, or restocking existing woodlands.

Trees planted for ornament, or for special purposes such as small shooting spinneys, orchards and arboreta, may need protection because quick establishment or 100 per cent success is paramount. Unfortunately, the lack of commercial basis for planting can also mean a limited budget and in consequence any protection needs not only to be effective, but as cheap as possible.

Full-scale deer fencing, though fully justified in many cases, is a very heavy capital expense and needs continual maintenance over 10 or 15 years. No fence is entirely effective, and it is therefore essential that provision is made to let enclosed deer out by means of leaps, and to cull out or manage those which take up residence inside.

Besides snow, flood and the deer themselves, the country walker is a potent factor in breaching deer fences. Rights of way have, of course, to be respected, but in deference to the elderly, the dog-owner and the vandal, any stile, ladder or gate designed to allow the public to pass must be massively constructed, very easy to surmount without injury, and very obvious. Otherwise holes will soon appear. Ladders at corners and other likely places will also be appreciated by the legitimate passer-by, beater and forest worker, for example. Dog-gates by stiles and ladders can be made quite cheaply. Where badgers are common, their habit of digging up fences put across traditional runs can be accommodated by a series of badger gates, as developed by the Forestry Commission.[9] These are not needless extra

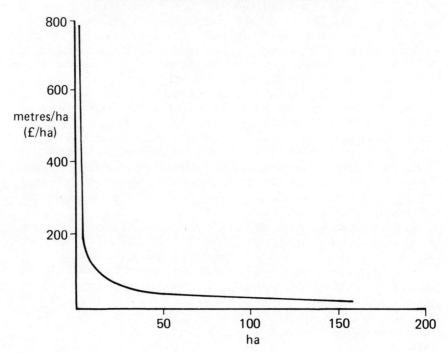

ROE DEER CONTROL AND RESTOCKING

expenses, but prudent and necessary measures to protect the deer fence and make it effective.

The design and erection of deer-proof fences is well covered in existing literature.[10] One can, however, see the most surprising variations, some of which render the fence in question completely ineffective. Deer prefer to creep through a fence than jump it unless they are driven, or chased by dogs. They can turn sideways to slip between horizontal wires, and even male deer with spreading antlers pass through a wire fence with a quick flick of the head, hardly checking their speed.

Bill Hamilton, who was responsible for the experimental deer farm at Glensaugh, stated that red deer can get through a gap of 20.3cm (8in) easily and can squeeze through 17.8cm (7in).[11] Drains under fences are open doors. Roe deer are so slim that they can penetrate almost any fence composed of long wires. Tension also is rarely maintained even with high-tensile spring steel wire, and soon there is sufficient slack for the larger deer to force their way in. Mesh of some sort is the only certain answer. Hinds in Scotland have the reputation of pushing their way eventually through any mesh fence open enough to admit their heads.

Of the types of netting available, woven or welded square mesh are the most durable. 7.5cm (3in) mesh wire netting is quite satisfactory, though fragile. Chain-link fencing has the merit of being unclimbable, but needs very sturdy posts and a reasonably level run to maintain an even tension. It is difficult to repair when damaged. Plastic netting was tried at one time, either full width or as a supplement above rabbit netting. Both were disastrous. Bucks became entangled in the full-width netting and not only strangled themselves, but in their struggles destroyed large sections of the fence. The half-width soon rotted under the influence of sunlight.

The following fence heights are generally accepted as providing 95 per cent protection.

Red deer	1.90m (6ft 4in)
small areas	1.70m (6ft 0in)
Fallow	1.70m (6ft 0in)
small areas	1.30m (4ft 3in)
Roe & muntjac	1.50m (4ft 3in)
small areas	1m (3ft 3in)

In all cases care must be taken that the effective height of the fence is not reduced, either by sag between posts, or by nearby banks or stumps off which the deer can jump.

Downfalls

On the large scale of Scottish afforestation, fences are inevitably erected across many minor deer paths, and also across their traditional migration routes, interfering with seasonal movements between hill and wintering ground. Besides the implications of this for the management of red deer on the deer forests, interference with movement patterns can increase the pressure on the fence, and therefore the likelihood of a mass break-in. Forestry blocks lying across these paths should be broken by downfalls, open ways by which the deer can pass on their way without piling up against the fence, to break it or die there as winter clamps down. Study of the block to be fenced and planted will determine the routes most favoured by the deer. Some at least should be incorporated into the downfalls.

The top fence on a hillside planting is always most vulnerable to pressure, and where possible the downfall should have a lead-in, that is to say the fence should funnel towards the entry to encourage travelling deer in the right direction. Cost and other considerations almost always determine the shape of a fence, even if the trees inside are given an irregular edge for landscape effect. Even so, re-entrants should be avoided if at all possible.

Small Enclosures

When faced with the need to plant up small areas, especially in or adjoining thick cover, protection is essential. The choice lies between conventional, temporary or electric fencing, individual tree guards or the use of deterrents. Often such small plots are supremely important for one reason or another, and warrant this additional expense to make sure as many trees as possible grow.

Windblow may leave small and irregularly shaped areas to be restocked. Where possible these should be enlarged by further felling to make reasonably sized clearings which can be economically deer fenced. Very small plots are probably better left until they can be incorporated into a larger planting scheme, but if immediate restocking is essential temporary fencing can be considered. Where roe only are present, the new planting needs to be protected until the leaders are above the 1.8m (3ft 6in) mark. This can be achieved quickly with hardwood whips, or in the case of transplants, by making use of temporary fencing which can be removed after three or four years for use elsewhere. Two-metre-high (6ft 6in) Weldmesh or woven wire fencing can be slung from the surrounding trees, and will survive two or even three moves. When erecting it, and even more when struggling to take it down again, a clear 3m (10ft) track on the fence line is almost essential. This technique is widely used on the Continent. It is very suitable for irregularly shaped areas, and deer are less likely to break into a round enclosure than one with straight sides.

At Eskdalemuir in Dumfriesshire Mr Ronnie Rose, Wildlife Officer for the Economic Forestry Group, has succeeded in establishing small hardwood groups inside one-metre-high (3ft 3in) sheep fences. These groups are little more than 20m (65ft) across, and Mr Rose says that the roe do not

bother to jump the fences as they would if the enclosures were bigger. The pioneering work that has been achieved in the Border hills under his direction is an example of how success can be achieved in reconciling wildlife management and large-scale commercial forestry. It should be said that part of his success is founded on keeping the roe density at a relatively low level so that the deer, even in winter, are not starving and desperate.

If the new trees have to be protected from rabbits a traditional fence will probably be necessary and in this case relatively small additional expense will make it deer-proof. All that needs to be done is to order all posts an extra 60cm (2ft) in height. The top long wire can then be used to carry wire netting 60cm (2ft) wide above the rabbit netting. Ensure that both runs of netting are effectively clipped together, otherwise deer charging the fence may burst through at the joint. In all deer fencing the long wires must be kept tightly strained. The Forestry Commission developed the use of high-tensile spring steel wire which, though awkward material to handle without the proper equipment, has simplified the construction of fences, and reduced the cost. A turn of the buckles is occasionally needed to maintain the tension. Due to its elasticity, a fence with spring steel long wires can withstand a degree of impact, from falling branches for instance, which would leave other fences sagging and useless.

Deer Leaps

Deer leaps are only just beginning to be recognised as an effective aid to fence maintenance and the reduction of damage. The day when they will be incorporated into deer fences as a matter of course is regrettably still distant. Why the evidence from nearly any deer-fenced area in Scotland of a deeply-trodden path made by the deer inside the fences should be disregarded is difficult to understand. Given an escape hatch, they are all too willing to get out. Inside they are a menace, outside a sporting asset. The cheapest solution by far is to let them out. If, because of an inefficient or poorly-maintained fence, female deer enter an enclosure and have their young inside, the likelihood is that the calves or fawns will be unable to jump out, and by the time they are big enough they will be hefted to the place and

unwilling to leave. A properly designed leap helps to prevent a breeding herd developing inside the fence.

A deer leap need not be expensive if it is put up at the same time as the fence. All that must be certain is that the design and siting ensures that the deer will use it. One common misunderstanding concerns the height of a leap. Many of the old-established deer parks had deer leaps, where the design can be studied. The main feature is that the jump-down is much lower than anyone would imagine necessary to stop a deer from jumping up and in again. This is most easily explained in terms of equitation. Riders will know that a solid obstacle on to which a horse has to jump is a much more formidable proposition than a fence or wall with ground level much the same on both sides. Once horse, or deer, has cleared the top of a fence, speed and gravity will get it down the other side. Jumping up on to a bank involves sufficient impulsion to bring the hind legs up, and to regain balance. Otherwise the animal will fall back.

For this reason 1.4m (4ft 6in) height is sufficient to deter a red deer, always provided that the wall is sheer, and that he does not have some advantage of ground, such as a bank, to assist his take off. The construction need not be expensive or complicated, nor the hole in the deer fence wider than 1m (3ft 3in). The top wire of a multi-strand fence can be left intact to preserve the tension, and rough boards can be nailed to adjoining fence posts to retain the earth which is to form the ramp. The ground can sometimes be dug away but even then boards must be used to prevent the wall becoming climbable, and drainage is essential to prevent the jump-down from turning into a pond.

The design of the ramp itself is vital. If instructions are given to the digger driver to make 'a ramp' he will make one at right angles to the fence, like those with which he is familiar, designed for loading tractors on to lorries. Ramps to lead deer to a leap must be made parallel with the fence with a gradual slope. Otherwise they will encounter the new barrier as they patrol the fence, make a detour and then carry on down the fence line. One wooden ramp in Scotland, beautifully made, but at right angles to the fence, had a well-trodden path *underneath* it, though the stags must have had to duck their heads. It was never used.

Placing a leap needs local knowledge, or at least understanding of deer behaviour. In hill ground the top fence, and especially the corners, are likely places for deer to attempt to escape. If the leap is to be constructed in an existing fence, the critical places will be self-evident. Putting a leap where it is easiest to get earth-moving machinery is tempting, but unlikely to be effective. In remote corners a ramp made of thinnings covered with turf is a good substitute, failing solid earth.

In areas liable to heavy snowfall, deer may walk in over the drifts. A light-weight hurdle should be made and hung nearby ready for use. The opening can then be closed in winter, and re-opened when the risk of snow has gone.

Some leaps are used almost at once. Others are discovered after a time. Should the response be slow, food can be put out to tempt the deer on to the ramp. If tracks prove that they are passing it by, a short low fence running back from the opening will help to channel them in.

In Austria, where the Alpine winters make red deer damage a problem, one owner has made use of leaps in an original fashion. A large proportion of the deer population is trapped each autumn. The top enclosure of a series of paddocks is regularly fed as winter approaches, and the deer are tempted to enter, either over leaps, or through self-shutting gates. One night's catch is driven into the adjoining paddock, where they are fed, and the catching pen is ready once more. When the snow finally melts, the gates are opened and the deer are free to wander in the mountains again.

A New Zealand deer farmer used a similar system of self-shutting gates to catch wild stock. As the pen was some distance away, he attached a device to the gate which released a homing pigeon when the gate slammed. He knew exactly when to arrive with his lorry!

Roe deer do not of course need the full height of 1.4m (4ft 6in) to deter them from jumping in, but they will use such a leap, and as other deer may be in the vicinity, it is as well to standardise. These deer can also be extracted from a fenced area by the use of a 'turnstile'. Two hurdles are made from closely spaced spruce tops so that the thin ends are free to flex individually. A hole is made in the fence where roe are trying to escape, and the two hurdles are set up in a vee-shape with their tips nearly touching at the apex. The deer force their way past, but are unable to pull back, or to get in from outside. A similar device can be made using short lengths of high-tensile spring steel wire in place of the spruce tops.

Stand-off Wires

Conventional deer fences, no matter what the basic design, can be demolished if two male deer find themselves on opposite sides during the rut. Knowing that neither is taking a great risk, like Konrad Lorenz's dogs in a similar position,[12] they fight with unusual ferocity. The only sufferer is the fence. This is a common occurrence in deer parks, where there are outlying bucks. The answer is a stand-off wire, about 60cm (2ft) from the ground level and 45cm (1ft 6in) from the main fence, on whichever side is convenient. This effectively stops the bucks from meshing their antlers through the fence and twisting about until it breaks. The wire can be barbed or electrified, but in the latter case the grass below it should be treated with total herbicide to prevent shorts. A high-intensity fencer unit is desirable.

Grids for Roads and Driveways

Deer of all species appear to respect the normal design of cattle grids, but a double width is prudent. Care must be taken with the installation, as well as a few points of design. The bars themselves should be round, not flat-topped, as should the bearers which take the weight. Red deer in Raby Park, Durham, regularly crossed one grid out of the park by walking between the bars, on the joist below. If really pushed, red or fallow could easily clear this distance, but seem very unwilling to do so. One Dorset stag used to get into the gardens by jumping a grid, but as he did this at night, nobody saw how he managed it. He always made the bars clatter, as if it was not a clean jump.

The well beneath the grid must be reasonably deep, and adequately drained to avoid it filling with water. Frost overnight would then give any animal safe passage. Snow can also be a problem, filling or covering over the bars. A gate over the grid is a safeguard for snowy districts, or, in emergency, flashing yellow traffic hazard lights can be used to warn the deer away until the thaw. An obvious point to remember is that the ends of the grid should be fairly close to the fence posts; shoulders which would be impassable to cattle may be wide enough for the deer. Small mammals will fall into the well and should be provided with an escape route either through the drain, or by making a sloping ramp to ground level.

Electric Fencing

A permanent multi-strand electric fence has been estimated to cost 46 per cent less than the equivalent fence in welded mesh, but according to the Forestry Commission's research team, practical considerations and higher maintenance swing the balance towards the latter.[13] However, where the plantation to be protected from deer is small, or long and narrow, electric fencing has its place.

The most effective type of energiser available in the U.K. was developed in New Zealand for sheep. This is powered from a mains supply or a heavy duty 12 volt battery. For really remote locations a wind-driven generator can be obtained which keeps the battery charged. A 5000 volt pulsing current is produced on safe amperage. Approximately 6km ($3\frac{3}{4}$ miles) can be electrified from one energiser. An annual application of herbicide below the wire is advisable. Such is the power of these units that minor short circuits, caused by wet grass touching the wires or wet snow building up on the insulators are burned off. Although electric fences may have disadvantages as permanent substitutes for traditional stock or deer fencing, their use as short-term protection has great attractions. Plantations only need to be protected from roe, fallow or muntjac for the first few years, indeed many can be left unguarded for the summer months, so that the fence units could have double use in agricultural areas, being returned to the farm during the strip grazing season.

One problem in connection with electric fencing is ensuring that the deer see the fence and investigate it, even at night. Farmers who use paddock grazing systems will know how much damage deer can do to their wires, breaking them before feeling the sting. In the 1970s a metallic light-reflecting tape was developed in Sweden which was briefly marketed here under the trade name of 'Glo-gard'. This tape was capable of carrying an electric current, and was clearly visible at all times. Experiments with Glo-gard showed enormous promise. An orchard in Dorset which had been regularly raided by roe was effectively protected by one strand of tape coupled to an ordinary fencer unit. Other trials were equally encouraging, but after some technical difficulties in Sweden this product was taken off the market. An improved type is now imported by Wolseley Webb Ltd (Electric Avenue, Whitton, Birmingham) and 4-Shot Ltd (119 Station Road, Beaconsfield, Bucks).

In the meantime, the Game Conservancy has been promoting experiments to discover alternative methods and materials to exploit the potential of electric fencing, especially for short-term or temporary use. So far no firm recommendations have emerged, but some interesting and successful trials have been made in various parts of the country. On the question of visibility, the wire is most likely to be broken where it is either right out in the open, like strip grazing, or stretched across deer runs in thick cover. In both cases they are likely to encounter the fence at speed.

Strip grazing fence wires are commonly made of three materials: orange plastic with a metallic strand; braided wire and high-tensile wire. Of these, the first is most likely to be troublesome. The plastic deteriorates in sunshine, and if a deer hits the fence the wire will either break, or in flexing violently, the metallic strip carrying the current may fracture without any external evidence of failure. Braided wire is much more robust. Recently, a novel system of temporary sheep fencing has been developed by Harry Ridley of Stockbridge (H. Ridley & Sons, Chilbolton Down, Stockbridge, Hants). This uses high-tensile wires, reels of which are dispensed and wound up again from a mechanical 'barrow'. A modified version for deer fencing has been developed, and shows considerable promise, in conjunction with a Gallagher energiser. Using this system, the wires can be kept taut, and the deer are less likely to break it or become entangled. Electrified sheep netting, on the other hand, seems irresistibly attractive, particularly to fallow bucks. Numerous cases have been reported of bucks going away with complete lengths wound round their antlers. The sheep escape and the buck strangles or starves, so the new system is doubly welcome.

Where the fence crosses deer paths or racks, strips of plastic sack can be attached to the wire to make it noticeable, especially when newly erected. Otherwise, the wire can be backed up with a length of orange hazard tape as is commonly used round holes in the road, building sites and the like. It is obtainable from builders' merchants in two forms – plain plastic, or with a patch of reflective material at intervals. The latter is considerably more expensive.

An alternative is to combine the electrified fence with some other barrier. If rabbit netting is needed round a plantation, the two can be effectively combined, but the electrified wires must be where the deer can investigate them. First experiments indicate that the electric fence should be about 45cm (1ft 6in) outside the rabbit netting, with three or four strands at 40cm (1ft 4in) (30cm [1ft] if muntjac are present) 70cm (2ft 4in) 1m (3ft 3in) and if necessary 1.3m (4ft 3in). Although all species of deer can jump a fence of this height, they appear to be unwilling to do so, once they are acquainted with its sting.

Five plantations on an estate in Hampshire were fenced in February 1981, using the Ridley system, modified for deer with the top strand height about 1.4m (4ft 6in), offset as suggested from a rabbit fence. Fallow, roe and muntjac were present, but even after the following winter not a single deer had got in. Curiously enough, one of these fences was never connected to an energiser, but was still effective. One assumes that painful experience had taught the local deer not to meddle. The fact that the work was done in a comparatively mild spring may have helped to train potential intruders to respect the fence at a time when they were not too desperate for food.

Most deer prefer to squeeze through or underneath wire fences although they are agile jumpers if need be. Unless chased, they usually stop and then cat-jump unless the crossing place is well-known and used. Anything new will be investigated. A damp nose making contact with 3000 volts, though perfectly safe, gives a lesson which will not easily be forgotten.

Deer damage is a perpetual nightmare to many gardeners, even in the inner suburbs. Full deer fencing is rarely possible because of the expense and the problem of gates, drives and so on, besides any reluctance to convert a garden into something resembling a prison camp. Electric fencing across the main deer access tracks can be unobtrusive and relatively cheap. Even if the road frontage and driveway of a typical suburban garden are left undefended, deer are less likely to enter on that side. In this sort of situation a mains-powered fencer unit is convenient and maintenance-free. Annual application of herbicide below the wire should not be forgotten, and the voltage tested regularly to check for short circuits. A meter should be used for this purpose. Testing with a blade of grass as one did with old-style fencers is definitely not recommended!

Electric fencing is still very much in an exploratory stage. If total exclusion is needed, then traditional methods may score. As a cheap means of deterring the majority of deer, especially over comparatively short periods, or to protect small areas, it is well worth considering. When the problem of visibility has been resolved, one or two strands may be found to be sufficient. In this event, the costs will be low enough to justify widespread use.

Individual Protection

Even if total fencing is not justified, anything out of the ordinary in a plantation, exotic or ornamental trees, standards and specimens, will receive more than their share of attention from deer and may need extra protection.

Our ancestors protected their parkland trees with substantial wrought-iron guards. They were rarely removed, and grew into the tree, as many an unsuspecting chain-saw operator has discovered. Nowadays, the cost would be prohibitive, and alternatives must be found in places where browsing pressure is severe. Horses and cattle have a prodigious reach, and being used to fences will strain and heave to get at the inviting twigs. Substantial structures are needed to resist them. Deer, fortunately are not so destructive; light netting is sufficient to protect young trees, but in choosing which method to use, care should be taken to avoid anything which fits tightly enough and lasts long enough to spoil the timber. Once the trees are growing well, the protectors will be hidden and forgotten.

Trees can be protected from fraying with a light stake close on either side, but this does not help against browsing. It is a useful method where standards are being planted. One stake will be needed in any case, and the leading shoots will already be out of reach. At one time the Forestry Commission developed a method of protecting poplar by slitting the bottom of a plastic sack and fitting it over the tree. A light stake on either side supported the sack, and kept it up off the ground, so that there was some

ventilation. This method was effective against roe, even if the visual impact was rather startling. Stakes and bags rotted away after three or four years, but by this time these fast-growing trees would no longer be vulnerable to damage. The wide spacing usual with poplar and their susceptibility to damage justified individual protection.

The spiral plastic guard developed to protect trees specifically from rabbits is now familiar, and exists in a variety of basic designs. None of them can be considered satisfactory against deer, with the possible exception of muntjac. The light-weight spirals can easily be hooked off by a roebuck. Indeed some roe and fallow bucks seem to take a delight in playing with them. Even rooks have been observed to unwind them, presumably in search of insects sheltering beneath.

Where roe or muntjac are the only species present, some of the heavier spirals, and other designs of split, perforated tube are more satisfactory. They do not, of course, protect from browsing. In an effort to stop deer from pushing these sleeves up and off the plants, foresters may be tempted to tie them on. Wire or plastic baler twine are very long-lasting materials. In at least one case an entire poplar plantation was ruined in this way. Most of the trees cracked off at the height of the tie, and remnants of plastic were still visible where the trees had been ringed.

Recently new materials[14] have become available which give excellent protection against the attacks of deer, rabbits and hares. Semi-rigid plastic netting is made up in rolls so that suitable lengths can be cut off to make the recommended 75mm (3in), 150mm (6in) and 300mm (12in) diameter guards. No. 1 size, 0.6m (2ft) wide, is designed to protect against rabbit and hare damage; No. 2 size, 1.2m (3ft 11in) wide for rabbits, hares and deer. Guards can also be made of larger diameter to give protection to bushy plants. The cut ends are joined to make a tube with the aid of pig-ring staples, as used in netting fencing, or they can be stapled to the supporting post with a stapling gun. Tubular guards are also available which may be used without a stake, but unless the trees are fairly large and stout they are liable to blow about in the wind, or bend over in heavy snow.

So far, no reports have come in of these plastic guards being eaten by rabbits, rats or grey squirrels, though the two latter species might be troublesome. According to the makers they are 'bio-degradable' or put more simply, they rot away in five to seven years, and thus do not need to be removed. The cost of netting guards is two or three times that of spirals but the protection they give is incomparably better. As a very high proportion of trees thus protected can be expected to survive, many fewer need to be planted. The admittedly high cost is therefore offset to some degree.

Plastic tree shelters are now in widespread use, mainly for broadleaved species. Tubular shelters are more resistant to deer attack than the square-section type, and the correct height should be chosen according to the deer species present: roe 1.2m [4ft]; fallow/sika 1.6–1.8m [5ft 4in–6ft]; red 1.8–2.0m [6ft–6ft 6in].[50] Shelters need the support of a stout stake. As well as protecting the tree from deer, hares and rabbits, trials with a variety of conifer and hardwood species have shown remarkable increases in growth rates because of the greenhouse effect inside the tube.

Wire netting has risen very steeply in price, which makes sleeves of this material expensive, in addition to the disadvantage mentioned earlier of growing-in. Second-hand wire is sometimes available in good enough condition for this purpose, which is economical and tempting, but not ideal. Welded mesh wire, being stiff, makes excellent temporary shields bent into circular guards, which do not need staking, at least at roe height, 1m (3ft 3in). Guards for fallow (1.5m [5ft]) and red deer (1.8m [6ft]) may get pushed or blown over. A local farmer who gave up battery hens made some good guards from the cage bottoms.

Books on forest protection from Europe illustrate many ingenious forms of tree protection, some home-made, others commercially available. Most of them are very time-consuming and would be out of the question given the current wage rates in this country. On a very small scale it might be worth experimenting with strips of aluminium foil on the leading shoots of spruce. Glassfibre has also been suggested on the lines of Christmas tree decorations, and human hair is claimed to have a marked deterrent effect. Getting enough for a large plantation would present difficulties, nor would the scenery be enhanced.

Chemical Deterrents

Anyone who has visited woodland in Germany or Austria will be familiar with the white paste which is smeared on the leading shoots of spruce every winter. The technique is so widely used that it is reasonable to wonder why the same thing is not done in this country, when so many complaints are made of browsing damage. Why indeed? A number of different products are on the market, and even with the longer and more severe winters abroad, there is no doubt that these deterrents are quite effective.

One administrative difference has a great deal to do with this question. On the Continent the shooting tenant pays for game damage, or for measures to prevent it, while here the forester is left to his own problems and solutions. Unless timber and shooting are both regarded as forest crops, the forester will see no advantage in spending extra cash defending his plantations when he would prefer to have no deer at all. Thus rather a negative attitude has grown up regarding the use of deterrents. Even so, the Forestry Commission do now advise that three or four, out of 60-odd deterrents tested, do have a place in minimising browsing damage in plantations which are too small to justify fencing.[15] That is to say less than 2 hectares (5 acres).

The majority of chemical deterrents are only suitable for use on dormant twigs and foliage. If used when the tree has flushed in the spring, growth may be severely checked. According to their consistency, deterrents can be sprayed, painted or smeared on the leading shoot. Spraying is quicker but less long-lasting. A number of tongs or rollers are marketed for large-scale work but failing them, rubber gloves and a square of plastic sponge to saturate the leader works surprisingly well. Five hundred plants per hour is easy to achieve in a plantation where access is fairly clear. Spraying would cover at least twice this number in the same time. The foliage must be dry, or the mixture will not adhere. Application of deterrents to dormant shoots is best done in November or December, just before the period of maximum risk, otherwise the effect may have worn off before the end of winter.

Newly-planted trees are the most attractive to deer. Speculating on the preference they show for transplants as against naturally grown trees, the late Sir Frank Fraser Darling gave the opinion that a transplant, being essentially a wounded plant, secreted pectins or other volatile substances which were sought out eagerly by deer.[16] Whatever the reason, trees newly brought from the nursery are particularly vulnerable to browsing by deer, hares and rabbits. In spite of this, one sees bundles of plants heeled in prior to planting *outside* the rabbit fence, presumably to keep them out of the way. One useful technique is to dip the bundles of plants in deterrent before heeling in or planting. Great care must however be taken to prevent the chemical coming into contact with the roots. The bundles must be left upside-down to drain, but of course not long enough to allow the roots to dry out.

The only deterrent which is recommended by the Forestry Commission for use on actively growing foliage is Fowikal, marketed by Berkshire Factors Ltd (London Road, Sunningdale, Ascot, Berks). Good results have been obtained against roe deer and rabbits. It is available in aerosol cans and also in bulk for spraying. The cans are very convenient for small areas, and in fact they are so quick and convenient that some foresters prefer to stand the higher cost rather than fill, use and clean out a knapsack sprayer. The effect is unlikely to last more than six weeks or so, though the manufacturers claim a longer period. In the case of roses, always a problem, applications should be made just as the leaves flush in spring, and again when the flower buds are ready to burst.

Two deterrents for winter use are recommended: Aaprotect (Midox Ltd of Smarden, Kent) and Cervacol (Berkshire Factors Ltd). Aaprotect can be used full strength for painting, dipping or spraying. Cervacol is more suitable for smearing.

For anyone of an experimental turn, trials with some of the continental home-made mixtures might be interesting. Ueckermann gives the following fascinating nostrums[14]:

45kg whiting
50 litres water
5 litres paraffin
600g adhesive

30kg whiting
20kg sand
4 litres linseed oil
100cc mineral or animal oil

40kg whiting
45 litres liquid manure (from cesspool)
15kg cowdung (fresh and creamy)

10 litres cattle blood
30kg whiting
5kg fishmeal
200g adhesive
2kg washed, sharp sand
20 litres liquid manure
4kg cowdung (as before)
35 litres water

Other ideas have centred on rancid seal oil and powdered glass or quartz. Some reasonable results were obtained twenty years ago with latex-based emulsion paint.

Not all deterrents need to be applied to the trees themselves. Various substances are disliked by deer, such as diesel oil, creosote, or the proprietary compound Renardine. Rags or string soaked in one or other will work for a short time, but the deer soon get used to them, and the smell must be changed. Mothballs, and that hoary chestnut lion dung, have had their adherents but proven results are still to seek. Judging by the way roe desert woodland where wild garlic flourishes, something might be tried in that direction.

Other Deterrents

Deer are adaptable animals. Part of their success lies in an ability to learn quickly whether something is dangerous or not. For this reason the majority of scaring devices only work for a short while before the deer disregard them completely.

All scarecrow-type ideas fall into this category, and unless they are frequently changed, have little effect. The same applies to noises. One can see roe lying and feeding within a short distance of even the most powerful

bird-scaring cannon once the initial impact has worn off. The other point is that deer feed late and early, when loud noises are likely to disturb local residents.

Some experiments were made by the Game Conservancy into the deterrent effect of a powerful flashing light. These showed enough promise to merit further work. Like cannon, there is the problem of disturbance unless the crop is remote from any houses.

The use of mirrors to deter deer from crossing roads by night has been tried in the New Forest, at Thetford in Norfolk and elsewhere. Small stainless steel plates or plastic reflectors are mounted on short posts at 45 degrees to the road, so that the headlight beams from approaching traffic flash a warning into the woods. Deer waiting to cross are at least kept back from the roadside, the risk being that one will cross safely, to be followed by the rest of the group regardless of traffic.

If the mirrors are sited carefully at known black spots, such as corners or blind crests, the accident rate can be materially reduced. Deer will continue to cross, but they will either wait for quiet times to do so, or change to places where motorists have a better chance to see them. Motorway planting has been very short-sighted in this respect. Where a run of woodland has been breached by the construction of the motorway, the likelihood of a wildlife crossing point exists. To plant trees on the embankment as is commonly done, brings animals to the very brink of the carriageway. The potential for serious accidents is increased enormously by this well-meaning but unimaginative action. Eighty-thousand accidents on roads in West Germany are caused annually by game, involving insurance claims in the region of 100 million Deutsch marks.

Section II

Deer Control

5 *Planning Effective Deer Control*

As well as giving forethought to the ways in which browsing and other damage may be avoided by manipulating forest operations, equal care should be given to making deer control as efficient as possible as a management exercise. Stalking is a time-consuming business and, whatever the size of the planting to be protected, the stalker needs to be able to use his time effectively.

Density

Allowing the population of deer to get too high leads inevitably to serious problems, no matter what devices are resorted to in attempts to reduce damage, short of the construction and maintenance of deer-proof fences in perpetuity. The stalker's main task is to prevent this and his efforts should be supported by management action to facilitate the task.

Deer density can only be adjusted within narrow limits where other deer-populated land adjoins. Even so, to keep numbers at a level even slightly below carrying capacity can make a fundamental difference both to the damage suffered and to the quality of antlers which are produced. If there are too many deer for the food supply, they will inevitably do damage. Two courses of action are open: to reduce the deer density; or to increase the food available. Artificial feeding is not only expensive, but can lead to bark stripping and other problems. However, increasing the natural browse supply may prove sound financial sense.

Scrub as Honey Pots

Under the heading of 'Weeding', the advantages of providing browse for the deer have been discussed. From the point of view of efficient control, scrub which attracts deer either to eat the twigs or to fray on the stems should be left or planted where the deer, thus preoccupied, can be seen, approached and, if appropriate, shot. Ride sides, stream banks if kept clear, rocky knolls and boggy or frosty pockets are obvious places, providing there is reasonable access so that they can be approached silently. Where there are large areas of unstalkable thicket, and little of the crop at risk, a reasonable harvest of adult bucks can be taken in succession, as replacements will be tempted out from more difficult territories. Deer hot-spots are also likely to be even more productive if a few bushes are planted on which they can browse. A list of trees, shrubs and crops to which deer are attracted and which can be used for this purpose, is given in the Reference Section and the subject is discussed more fully in Chapter 8.

When open ground is being afforested, any hardwoods intended as deer browse should be put in at the same time as the main planting, so that they are established when deer colonise the new trees. If hares or rabbits are present, or if the area is subject to incursions by red deer, they need protection until they are growing strongly.

Open Spaces

The need for open spaces within the wood or forest in which deer can be seen and controlled is slowly becoming acknowledged. Despite this, blanket planting continues, leaving only the narrowest rides and paths. This is short-sighted from the point of view of future deer control, and for game shooting, should this be one of the activities in the area. For access and timber extraction the forester also needs dry, easily maintained roads. When the ground is laid out it is difficult to visualise how quickly a nine- or ten-metre ($\frac{1}{2}$ chain) ride will close in. Nor, at that stage, will the need for deer control be at all pressing. Roe deer may not immediately colonise the ground. Red deer will have to be excluded by a fence where they are present.

In any case, the trees are so small that any deer can be spied and dealt with. Only later when few rides remain passable, when the trees have grown high enough to hide the deer and the expensive fence has been breached in a storm, does the need for control start, and the lack of provision for it become apparent. By this time making openings will be doubly difficult because of the risk of precipitating windblow, and the investment which the unwanted trees already represent. There is no more difficult thing than removing trees once planted, no matter what plans were made in that direction originally.

In the early years, all the stalker needs is a network of access tracks cut once a year with a scrub-cutter to allow him to walk freely and quietly. As the trees start to grow up, even narrow openings are invaluable. Some years ago a shortage of stock in several nurseries resulted in some foresters leaving every tenth row unplanted as an economy. This practice continued until recently. Roe stalkers made good use of this additional visibility in the early and vulnerable years of such plantations. Later, of course, they grew in, as do many other rides which seemed wastefully large at the time of planting. One broad ride is worth much more than a network of tunnels in the greenery, though the acreage may be similar. Minimum maintenance, in the form of cutting or fertilising, is likely to produce returns in venison far outweighing the cost.

Deer control has to continue throughout the rotation. Disease or windblow may strike at any time making piecemeal replanting necessary. Even when production starts, the clearfell areas are unlikely to exceed 50 hectares (120 acres) or so, to which the deer will be attracted. Unless provision is made originally in the layout to permit continued and efficient control, the heavy expense of fencing such areas has to be faced.

Night shooting of deer, which to many troubled foresters seems a facile answer, is no solution (*see* Chapter 13). Open spaces, whether natural or planned, whether multi-purpose, such as for extraction or fire rides, or specially made for deer control, are essential in large-scale forestry. Nor is one large open space any substitute for many small clearings scattered throughout the area. Deer will soon learn that an open space is dangerous if they are repeatedly attacked there.

The design of deer control areas and the use to be made of natural features is further explored in Chapter 7 under 'Forest Design for Deer Control'.

Flexibility

Planning for efficient deer control inevitably demands a scheme of management, with culling targets laid down for each species, sex and age-class. These are based on estimates of the total population, the sex ratio and reproductive rate. To keep deer numbers stable, the annual surplus, less natural mortality, is taken. If the population has to be reduced, for example because of excessive damage to vulnerable plantations, the number of females culled is increased to cut down the fawn crop. So far so good, except for the large numbers of variable or unknown factors in the calculation. Natural mortality, for instance, varies widely from one year to another. Movement due to weather or disturbance can suddenly inflate deer numbers, or as quickly diminish them. Farming operations, be it a fashion for autumn-sown corn or routine pesticide spraying, can attract deer from a wide area, or banish them from the fields. Poaching can also reduce deer numbers literally overnight. Not only are animals taken, often by barbarous methods, but some are left to die and the remainder are driven out of their normal habits by constant harrassment. The shooting plan has to be adjusted in consequence.

If culling targets are set, as is desirable, they should never be taken as immutable. The larger the organisation involved, the greater the risk that returns of deer numbers are regarded almost in the same way as money. Insisting on a stalker achieving his full quota of does when half the population has already been poached is as pointless as it is inefficient. His time would be better spent elsewhere – or on poacher patrol. Equally, if he finds more deer on the ground than expected, the cull can be re-considered and increased: Preferably in consultation with any adjoining owners whose deer for some reason may have gone astray.

An over-mathematical approach to fixing culling levels may also prove misleading. For example, one usually assumes that roe does have about 1.7 young annually, of which 50 per cent die or emigrate in the first year. Therefore, in a population of 1:1 sex ratio, 100 roe will produce 42.5 yearlings. However, roe are virtually impossible to count accurately. The sex ratio is more likely to be 1:1.5 male to female and mortality plus emigration depends on the degree of exploitation. The more that are shot, the less die or are driven out, up to a level where the true reproductive rate is exceeded. At this point the normal spring cast-out of surplus juveniles is likely to be replaced by immigration from neighbouring woods. Roe, as a typical prey species, are thus highly resistant to predation. Effective plans have to be based on as good information as can be obtained, but should never lose a degree of trial-and-error flexibility.

One exception to this rule needs to be mentioned. Having fixed a reasonable doe cull, the early part of the season may produce a disastrous lack of success. All manner of good reasons for reducing the cull will come to mind, but in the absence of really hard information, they should be resisted. Two factors contribute towards deer being often hard to find in November and December. One is disturbance due to pheasant shooting, which can induce them to change their ground, particularly in the case of fallow. The other is the phenomenon known as inappetence, which means that during the winter months the metabolism of the deer slows down.[17] Their need for food is accordingly adjusted. All species can be relatively inactive and feed very little, without losing condition as one would expect. After Christmas they are active once again as the females become heavier in young, and in the case of roebucks the demands of territory and antler growth reassert themselves. Deer that one had assumed to be lost or poached in the autumn are suddenly to be seen again. Only a short time remains to achieve the original target before the end of the season.

Liaison

The advantage of a free and regular exchange of ideas and information between people involved in different aspects of land management needs no emphasis. The stalker, because he is about at odd hours, can help the gamekeeper by letting him know of any suspicious characters or vehicles seen. On the other hand, nothing can be worse for the pheasant keeper than to hear an unexplained shot which he will feel obliged to investigate. He is entitled to know each time the stalker is operating. Passing too near a release pen in late summer or autumn and thus putting young pheasants off roost last thing at night should also be scrupulously avoided.

Discussion between stalker and forester can often avoid conflict or unnecessary damage. Indeed, during the rut when stalking may take place during the day, and in the short winter days of the doe season, the stalker must know where men will be working, or walking to their work. The farm manager or whoever is responsible for day-to-day operations needs the stalker's active collaboration, just as he can, by thoughtless or unexpected action, make the stalker's job more difficult. Delaying stubble burning for just one day after combining may expose deer that have been living in the corn. On the other hand, nothing can be more embarrassing than taking a paying guest out to shoot a buck which has been seen every night in a certain field, only to find on arrival that the field has just been sprayed, and therefore is unattractive to deer. The arrival of a flock of sheep has the same effect.

Forward Planning

Long-established woodland areas under a consistent management regime usually provide a stable environment for deer. As one parcel is felled, others are growing up. The deer population is unlikely to fluctuate greatly.

In sharp contrast to this traditional picture, we now have a very large proportion of even-aged plantations, due to the post-war replanting and afforestation programme. In these, rapid and fundamental changes to the habitat take place in a comparatively short time. Bare ground gives way to thicket and in due course to semi-mature woodland. Such changes not only affect the food supply, and thus the deer carrying capacity, but make a forest block successively more suitable for different species.

Thus one may expect early colonisation after planting by roe or muntjac, their numbers rising quickly to a peak and falling again as the ground vegetation is killed out by the closing canopy. Later a partial replacement by red, fallow or sika may be anticipated, depending on their local distribution.

The implications of these changes in population in relation to damage have already been discussed, but the long-term effects on forest and deer management need to be considered.

Clearly, if a deer population is in decline because the food supply is diminishing, browsing pressure will be severe in any nearby plantations still at a vulnerable stage. Control measures should attempt to anticipate the deterioration in habitat, by reducing the population to conform with the available food. If revenue has been sought through letting roe stalking, the numbers of bucks shot each year can be expected to decline as the canopy closes in an extensive even-aged plantation. However, thinning especially of larch, pine or hardwood crops, can allow new ground vegetation to develop and increase the holding capacity once more.

Apart from the basic questions of forest design best tackled at the planning stage, outline plans for deer management should be reviewed periodically in accordance with the five-year forestry plan. From this the likely trend in population and holding capacity can be judged, and culling targets adjusted to conform. Maintenance of a deer population in defiance of a reduction in natural food will lead both to damage and to deterioration of deer body weight and antler quality unless alternative feed or browse is provided.

6 *Stalker Efficiency through Management*

The stalker himself, if he is a professional, is the most expensive item in any deer management budget. If he is a trained amateur, he can be the most valuable! In either case every effort must be made to see that his time is spent as usefully and productively as possible. Comparisons are seldom fair, but the enormous difference in performance between extremes can be seen in the example confirmed by J. Davies, Conservator S.W.(S.) of 19 full-time Forestry Commission rangers in Galloway who each averaged 18 red deer and 24 roe deer per annum, shooting in and out of season, though admittedly they had subsidiary duties.[18] Their performance compares poorly with two stalkers on separate estates in the North of Scotland. Without the benefit of teamwork, one of them accounted for 90 red deer and 20 roe over 12 months in blanket-planted Sitka spruce. None were shot at night or out of the legal season. The other, equally legally, shot 73 roe does between October 21 and November 30 1981, and 150 before the end of the season. Without any reflection on the individuals concerned, the variation in efficiency between these two examples shows what potential exists for reducing protection costs if skill and devotion is backed up by active and intelligent direction and management.

The profession of deer stalker is a lonely one, needing the greatest capacity to work long, broken and antisocial hours without supervision. People attracted to this life tend to be individualists, often enthusiasts. The woodland manager, while valuing these qualities, should neither rely on enthusiasm without support, nor allow individualism to get out of hand.

The same professional approach needs to be built up as is found among the best hill-stalkers in Scotland. Woodland stalking is a year-round activity in most areas because of the presence of more than one species of deer. A stalker can become stale without some break from shooting, and some deadline in each year towards which he can work. To impose actual supervision is an insult, but he needs to feel that his work has the lively interest and approval of his employer.

The stalker's needs can be summarised as follows:

    Purpose
    Direction
    Training
    Equipment

Purpose

The stalker needs to feel involved as much in the conservation and study of deer as he is in protecting the forest crop. It is soul-destroying to be ordered out to kill, and to have no other yardstick for success than the tally of carcases

at the week's end. That is not to say that severe limitation or even elimination of a population may not form part of the stalker's duties from time to time, but the reason needs to be clear to him, as well as the chances of achieving what he is asked to do. Callous killers do exist, but they do not make good stalkers. Knowledge and understanding of wildlife on the part of the stalker is necessary for consistently good results. He needs to be part of the process of management, not just a tool to be used according to issued orders.

Attempting to count small deer in thick woodland by observation is often misleading. As a more accurate alternative, the technique of pellet group analysis shows promise.[51] Deer behaviour can be studied at leisure, a very educational process, and unproductive parts of the wood can be thoroughly explored with an eye perhaps to making a clearing or erecting new high seats. Even though accurate census figures are really a myth, useful population trends can be established by employing the same techniques each spring and comparing the results from one year to another. Once the deer population is under reasonable control, the introduction of one or more stalking tenants can be considered. Not only does this bring in welcome cash, but the stalker is given a goal – the location of suitable bucks or stags, and a deadline – the arrival date of his stalking guests.

He will automatically plan his activities against the need to have everything ready by the critical day, and measure his abilities by the relative success of his guests. Many visitors to this country are extremely keen and knowledgeable, and they will certainly want to look at the past year's records. What better motive to keep them up, and demonstrate that a difficult and demanding job is being well done. Small tasks, such as clearing stalking paths and pruning round high seats, to say nothing of making sure that the ladders up to them are entirely safe, become urgent in the run-up to the visitor season.

If stalkers are not consulted when new planting is being planned, both technical and local knowledge is being thrown away. Such action is also disheartening in the extreme to the stalker, who feels not only that his professionalism and expertise are not being fully valued, but that his work is being made more difficult, less efficient. Brought into the discussion, he will be able to point out the places where damage is likely, the hot-spots and other critical areas better left unplanted, the best locations for deer leaps, and so on. The aspirations and problems of the forestry side will also be clearer to him and easier to understand and support.

Continuity of work is desirable, not only from the point of view of venison marketing, but because of the forest protection element in deer control. Experienced and productive stalkers, amateur or professional, need to have a reasonably even culling target from one year to the next, otherwise they may have departed elsewhere when an emergency or a new peak of work demands their attention. The worst problem is a large block of even-aged plantations, which needs an immense amount of supervision by the stalker in the first five or ten years after planting. The pressure on him then tends to ease until wind damage or clear felling produces another peak, and if he has in the meantime gone elsewhere, and the deer population has built up uncontrolled, damage will be inevitable and severe before new staff can be found and trained. Far better to prevent the build-up and retain staff by facilitating deer control through and after the thicket stage by employing the techniques of design and planning which are outlined in the next chapter. The expenses can be largely offset by proper marketing of venison and sport. Assistance may also be offered to neighbouring woodland owners who are likely to have suffered from a population increase caused by the deer spreading out from the main forest block as it becomes less congenial to them.

Direction

Having an employee whose work may be little understood, and whose hours are different from his colleagues, places a strain on management which can lead to the stalker becoming estranged and isolated, or the victim or remorseless exploitation. The mere sight of one worker digging his garden or otherwise amusing himself when others are hard at work is enough to make any employer search in his mind for some task for idle hands. By mid-morning in summer a roe stalker will probably have worked eight or nine hours already, with the prospect of another shift in the evening. He is entitled to his limited leisure. On the other hand, there is no occupation more easily exploitable by a lazy man, because of the lack either of set hours or specific work which allows him to be challenged.

Allowing for the vagaries of deer behaviour and weather, it is still possible to set out a stalker's duties within reasonable limits. A seasonal work calendar highlights peak periods for each task and avoids conflict or competition for his time. It should be coupled to a carefully written job specification (*see* Reference Section). A weekly diary, particularly for the younger man, allows the manager to have some written notes on the past week's work and gives him space for written orders, no matter how general, for the next. Being obliged to set out how each day is spent is in itself good self-discipline. In addition, any claims to have been in such a place at such a time can be checked occasionally.

To ask for some account of work done each pay day cannot be unreasonable, but detailing the stalker's hours as if he were a factory worker is out of the question. That decision must be his alone from day to day.

Instructions Name................... **For week ending**....................
to Stalker

Signed...................
Date...................

Stalker's   **Week**
Diary   **Name**......................   **Beat**.........................   **Ending**...................

	Areas visited	Time spent to nearest $\frac{1}{4}$ day	Details	Remarks
Mon				
Tues				
Wed				
Thur				
Fri				

Seasonal work calendar   In order to identify the peaks which inevitably occur in stalking work, and to slot in other duties between them, a seasonal work calendar should be prepared, separating out different aspects of the job, allocating a certain number of weeks each month as appropriate and either adding other duties in easy months, or making sure that no unnecessary burdens are imposed at times when stalking has to take precedence.

The table shows a simple lay-out, with an example of how one man's time might be divided between roe stalking and caring for a small grouse moor. It will be seen that by careful timing, butt-building has been planned to

STALKER'S SEASONAL WORK CALENDAR

Name . . . .

ESSENTIAL DUTIES	A	M	J	J	A	S	O	N	D	J	F	M
Roe bucks												
Roe does												
Visitor stalkers												
Heather burning												
Butt maintenance												
Grouse duties												
Fox control												

coincide with a difficult period in the buck season at the end of June, but allows for three weeks' stalking after that, finishing at 12 August. In the south, any squirrel control is often undertaken by stalkers. Where Warfarin is a legitimate method of control, the hoppers can be set up, the most time-consuming job, in late March before the start of buck stalking. Keeping them topped up is easily combined with stalking.

Other tasks of wildlife control, whether for the benefit of the forest itself or that of neighbours, like the control of hooded crows and foxes in Highland areas, may also be undertaken at times. Points such as these can be adjusted on the chart, helping to smooth out the peaks. If everyone knows that the work has been carefully planned, the deer stalker can get on with his work without being at the beck and call of other departments when he is at full stretch.

Regular contact between the stalker and everybody involved is vital. He benefits by building up a good 'bush telegraph' to report deer sightings, damage or the activities of suspicious characters. The farm and forest staff and tenant farmers begin to feel that they have an active friend, not a little-known and rarely-seen presence whom they suspect of keeping a private zoo at their expense.

A map set up on the farm office wall, with pins to indicate deer information will interest and involve everyone on the staff, *provided it is cleared completely and re-started once a year*. Simple progress charts giving the planned cull for different parts of the estate, and progress to date are visual indications of success at a job which mostly takes place when others are asleep.

Although most stalking is best done alone, there are times when team-work pays handsomely. Doe control is a good example. Plans for stalkers to work as a team can be made from time to time.

Training

Stalkers may be born, not made, but even given aptitude and keenness, a potential stalker cannot be expected to spring fully armed and trained from the soil. Woodland stalking in this country is a fairly new development, so we do not yet have the benefit of stalker's sons coming along with the advantage of having grown up in the profession. The old tradition of shotgun drives and snaring was swept away by public opinion after the Second World War, to be replaced at first by a small band of dedicated enthusiasts, many of whom spent an enormous amount of their time demonstrating that humane deer control with the rifle was indeed a practical alternative. Much of their work was done for nothing, as a service to landowners and farmers, and the value of their pioneering work should be recognised. They laid down the basis of our present approach to deer management, biologically-based, and orientated towards crop protection and the maintenance of healthy stock. In many ways this is in stark contrast to the continental tradition of emphasis on trophy quality. Even so, there are roe populations in Britain where good management has resulted in the production of first class 'trophy' bucks.

Stalkers, therefore, have to be trained in the techniques of woodland deer management before they can do the job efficiently. The development of low-cost woodland stalkers courses by the British Deer Society leading up to Stalkers Competence Certificates at National and Advanced levels has been widely welcomed. Students on these courses are inspired with new enthusiasm and a professional approach to the business of deer management, whether they are full-time or hobby stalkers. One point must not be forgotten on this score. It is no use training a man if his immediate supervisor is out of sympathy with the whole idea. More than one trainee has returned to his forest at the end of a course to have all his keenness killed in the first five minutes by blank opposition to change. Direction has to go all the way down the chain of command before stalker training is considered.

The correct sequence is first for the estate or forest policy to be decided and the priorities of management defined. Then this policy should be explained to immediate supervisors so that deer control forms an integral part of forest protection and production, rather than a separate and possibly conflicting activity.

Contact between stalkers in an area should be fostered, to get a free exchange of ideas, as well as to co-ordinate management plans or plan joint action against poachers. Social gatherings will supplement more formal meetings between landowners, although the stalkers will attend these as well. The trifling expense of laying on a target shoot, a barbecue or an evening of beer and skittles will be appreciated by men whose job is lonely, and will bear worthwhile dividends to the estates involved.

Deer management in this country is in a state of rapid development. Re-training by means of attendance at Deer Society meets or short refresher courses by the Game Conservancy is also well worth while. If owners, land agents and foresters can also spare the time to attend, deer work can be assimilated more quickly and smoothly as an integral part of land use on the estate.

Equipment

Very few items of stalking equipment are at all costly, and most are long-lasting. A serviceable rifle should not wear out for years if it is properly looked after, yet two or three red deer carcases will purchase one. A telescopic sight, the only tool which must be of the highest quality, will cost about the same, and will quickly repay the investment by extending accurate shooting hours into the twilight, when woodland deer tend to be on the move. One missed chance because the 'scope has misted up or changed zero will throw away the difference between a cheap instrument and one which is well made and reliable.

Not so long ago the most astonishing weapons were resurrected from dusty gun cupboards as 'good enough to knock over a roe'. Fortunately the provisions of the Deer Act and withdrawal of many obsolete calibres from ammunition makers' catalogues has banished most of those old gaspipes, and a stalker can expect to use a modern, accurate rifle. Many use their own, in which case an allowance is appropriate. Other equipment need not involve great expense. Some can be simply made or contrived, but a penny-pinching approach to the few items a stalker really needs is bad man-management. Detailed suggestions on fixed and small equipment are given in Chapter 10. Here, we are only concerned with the added drive and efficiency of a well-equipped stalker.

7 Forest Design for Deer Control

Theodore Van Dyke, who wrote one of the very few really practical books of instruction on stalking,[19] said that the most difficult part of stalking is actually to see a deer at all. If the stalker's job is to be made easier, there must be places in the forest where deer can be seen, where the deer have some reason to go, and where the stalker can approach them reasonably easily. An additional element, especially with red deer, is the ease with which a shot deer can be got to the nearest road.

The ideal situation from the point of view of deer management must first be defined, and then matched as far as possible to the needs of forestry itself, and of other elements in the use of forested land, such as recreation, wildlife conservation, visual amenity (landscape), fishing and so on.

Large-Scale Forests

Purely from the standpoint of deer management in extensive woodland, the basic need is for areas where deer can feed and sun themselves in relative peace. One large clearing is not enough. All forests are subject to disturbance, by the forest staff themselves, maybe a shooting tenant, ramblers and the like – not to mention poachers. If the deer are repeatedly put off their one feeding place, they will be forced to subsist on what the trees provide, and damage will result. If on the other hand they have a number of alternative areas, one is certain to be quiet if they are driven off another. Roe deer are territorial and very static all summer. Only one or two of the local bucks will show up in each open space. For this species in particular, a number of small feeding areas should be planned and maintained, interconnected with paths and tracks for easy, silent access.

Some ideal places have already been mentioned – the deer hot-spots, where some vagary of wind, sun or feeding makes a focal point. Stream banks are favourite places or where an old cottage garden or abandoned fields have left a residue of better feeding. Small outcrops of mineral soil are preferred in a wilderness of acid peat.

Work in the Border forests has shown how many unexpected holes occur naturally in what appears from the forest roads to be continuous dark canopy. Indeed there is a school of thought that nature is the best architect of the forest: that frost, poor soil conditions or chance mishaps to the trees will create sufficient 'deer clearings', just as the variety of soil types will determine what is planted, and thus the visual effect. On neither count is this *laissez-faire* approach sufficient, though good use can and must be made of any natural spaces which develop. Long before then the needs of management should have been foreseen and provision made for them in the overall forest plan.

Some places are naturally attractive to deer. Others have to be developed – perhaps by coppicing overgrown shrubs for browse – improved by management of the sward, or created specially, either through planning as part of an afforestation project, or by cutting out clearings in existing woodland. If no feed exists already, shrubs or arable crops will probably have to be planted to hold the deer in them.

A certain minimum size of forest clearing is necessary to avoid the deer eating out the coppice regrowth completely before it has time to give its proper yield. A minimum of 4 hectares (10 acres) has been recommended for red deer, and about 1 hectare (2.5 acres) for roe.[20] Smaller areas than this may be satisfactory if there are enough of them scattered through the woodland. However, if one is found to be browsed too heavily to get satisfactory regeneration, it should, wherever possible, be increased in size, or another created not too far away. The problem is that while roe are territorial, avoiding heavy concentrations of deer on the clearing except during the winter, red and fallow deer may pick on one and demolish it.

When overgrown coppice is cut down, it is advisable to leave the lop-and-top piled on the stumps to give the new shoots some protection.

The maintenance of these 'honey pots' must be kept to a minimum, and planting should be kept to species which will not become forest weeds, or grow large enough to hamper future operations such as timber extraction. Limited maintenance costs will be amply repaid in terms of venison sold, damage prevented, and possibly enhanced sporting rent.

Deer control is by no means alone in demanding a certain proportion of open space in the forest. Modern forest operations need hard, dry roads, with bays for temporary storage of produce and for manoeuvring heavy machines. Extraction routes become damp and easily rutted if they are allowed to become overgrown so that the surface never dries. Sufficient width should be allowed in the original planting to compensate for gradual loss as the trees grow and develop lateral branches. The trouble is that such a roadline looks enormous when the trees are small. The temptation is to plant nearly up to the road side, with a vague intention of taking out several rows at first thinning. This rarely happens, and by that time the road surface has probably already been destroyed. Main routes in a large forest block should be a minimum of 20m (1 chain) wide, either throughout their length, or at least at intervals to make long bays, or glades. The loss of plantable land will be made up by ease of working and by the contribution these glades can make to deer control if properly managed. With 8m (25ft) or so each side of the access track, the verges will become reservoirs for the natural flora of the district, which might otherwise be shaded out, and cover will be provided for many ground-nesting birds.[21]

In areas with abundant ground vegetation the shrub growth will need to be topped every two years. Where no browse occurs naturally, it will have to be planted.

As broad rides have the approval of the natural historian and conservationist, so the fisherman and landscape specialists support the deer manager in demanding that watercourses should be left unplanted. The catchment areas of many of our most important rivers are being planted up, with potentially serious effects on the acidity of the headwaters and spawning redds. Harriman and Morrison, in a study of moorland streams in Scotland,[22] found that the physical and chemical effects of intensive afforestation can result in the reduction, and in some cases the loss, of salmonid fish from streams draining some forest catchments. These points have been recognised in the Forestry Commission's policy statement, *The Forestry Commission & Conservation*:

The edges of plantations, both internal and external often provide good wildlife habitats. . . . Margins of plantations alongside roads, paths streams and open glades are left as irregular as possible, and special attention is given to protecting natural features such as streams and other areas of water, gullies and screes.

This was followed by the publication by the Forestry Commission of Dr D.H. Mills' booklet *The Management of Forest Streams*[23] in which he states:

The widths of the reserve areas of vegetation will vary with the landform but as a rough guide the overall width (both sides) could be 10 times the width of the stream, up to a maximum of 30 metres overall.

Within the reserve areas tree planting should be kept to the minimum required for landscape reasons.

The banks of water courses should in fact be left unplanted to a distance of at least 30m (100ft) from the stream, yet one sees few signs of actual progress in this direction. There are, however, notable exceptions, such as the Eskdalemuir forest administered by the Economic Forestry Group.

Besides the benefit to fish, unplanted stream banks make a welcome break in the continuous canopy of an even-aged forest, following a natural, and therefore harmonious, line downhill. Vistas are opened up where they are intersected by forest roads to be enjoyed by ramblers in the years ahead, and great diversity will be added to the forest wildlife. If steep banks are planted despite this, the timber will be costly to extract.

As soon as the canopy closes, use by deer of the stream banks will intensify, and any planting of browse should be well established by that stage. In well-roaded forest blocks, 150 metres up- and down-hill of each intersection between stream and ride should be planned, planted and managed as a deer control or observation clearing. Where intersections are few, stalking paths can be made to viewpoints from which lengths of the stream can be spied. Otherwise the deer will have to be approached by stalking along the banks. Unless there are occasional bends in the stream, or other obstacles behind which the stalker can creep, willow clumps can be planted at intervals which will shield him, as well as feeding the deer.

Other natural features can be exploited in the same way, preference being given to ground less suitable for planting, such as rocky knolls or frost hollows. The upper edge of any hill planting ought to have an irregular line in order to harmonise with the landscape, even if the fence containing it is straight. The strip of open ground between trees and fence is very likely to attract deer, and with a little management can be made into a productive haven, even if it is only enjoyed by younger and fitter stalkers!

On lower ground, the margin of ponds and lakes can be embellished with shrubs and serve the same purpose, provided that the timber crop is not allowed to crowd down to the water's edge.

Another technique which will greatly improve the appearance of a large conifer block is to plant patches of pure larch at intervals where the soil permits. These should not be small enough to attract serious damage, say more than 2 hectares (5 acres) each, and adjoining a path so that they can be approached silently. When the surrounding spruce or pine is black and impenetrable, the larch will already be nearing first thinning. After this

operation enough sun will reach the ground to encourage the undergrowth to develop and the whole stand becomes a feeding area without loss of crop. A small amount of brashing will give plenty of visibility for the deerstalker, and each subsequent thinning will improve it. Something of the same sort can be done alongside some rides, to increase their apparent width and to create better feeding for the deer where they can be seen.

Some wide fire breaks can in fact be too open to be attractive to deer. The wind sweeps up and down them, there is little to eat, and if the stalker does see a deer crossing, it will either be gone too quickly to approach, or he will be spotted because of the lack of cover. As the crop grows older these fire breaks lose their effectiveness, and can be replanned to serve the needs of deer management. By planting transverse blocks of trees at 150m intervals a series of glades are created which can be stalked one after the other. If the blocks include a proportion of edible browse species, deer will linger rather than moving through to some more luscious, and probably inaccessible, feeding place.

In an established forest, nothing can take the place of thorough exploration. The most unexpected and useful clear spaces may be found in what appear to be even-aged and continuous stands. All the streams should be walked, all hollows investigated. A large-scale map will indicate likely places which are invisible behind a wall of conifers. Mosaic maps made from aerial photography are sometimes available, or even actual photographs taken from the air. Nobody really knows a forest until he has seen it from above. No chance should be missed of looking down on to woodland, no matter how familiar it may be from ground level. The local flying club is worth contacting, and sometimes aircraft will be in use locally for spraying or spreading fertiliser. Fifteen minutes' flying time will cover a great deal of ground, and cost comparatively little.

Once a suitable clearing has been found, an approach path has to be cut through the surrounding trees from the nearest ride. Maybe some scrub will have to be coppiced, a few willows planted or a high seat built to make the site really useful.

One artificial feature which is a gift to the deer manager is a power line across the forest. The electricity authority will insist on a minimum width left clear beneath the wires which can be utilised by fertilising or reseeding strips to make deer lawns, planted at intervals with low-growing shrubs, or even cultivated and fenced off for winter feed crops.

Faced with an existing blanket-planted forest, entirely devoid of natural openings which could be used or improved, consideration will have to be given to making them in the crop. Clearly the minimum sacrifice of growing trees must be decided on, avoiding any risk of windblow through letting the wind into a stand. Settling the location of any new clearing depends on the points already discussed: they should be made in places where deer go, where they linger because of some attractive feed, and where the stalker can get to them easily and quietly.

By no means all the standing crop needs to be removed. In fact nearly a complete stocking at final crop spacing may sometimes be left. While the canopy must be interrupted to let in the sunshine, a certain number of trees scattered over the area makes it more attractive. Most of them will need to be high pruned. The very term 'deer lawn' is a complete misnomer. Wide open spaces spell danger to woodland deer. They feel safer where there is a straggle of trees or bushes, and while the larger species will graze on grass *provided it is less than 10cm (4in) high*, roe will only do so if there is no alternative. A 'deer lawn' for roe needs to have the appearance of a failed plantation, or rather of a failed arboretum. They find a great attraction in anything out of the ordinary.

Any sort of opening, if it is to be used for observation or control, needs to be a certain length from the spying or firing point. Otherwise the stalker is at too close quarters to his quarry, and any movement or noise will give him away. Sometimes a small clearing can be overlooked from a knoll or high seat in convenient rifle range, say 110 metres (120 yards) to the farther edge. Otherwise a pear-shaped area the same distance from end to end is ideal, with a high seat or other shooting point at the narrow end. Burn-side clearings made on the intersection with a forest road may extend 100 metres or so in both directions, but if red deer are the quarry and the stalker is single-handed he will only shoot uphill from the road!

The need for openings within the forest is, in theory, well known. Theory is not, however, being translated into practice, as has been mentioned. The problem is only partly due to a failure among foresters to understand the desirability or the need to make sacrifices of plantable land, as they see it, whether to landscape or wildlife conservation, to fishing or to deer management – though it bears a part.

The other side can be blamed on the courage of the average forestry ploughman. Given an area to plough, he will plough everything he dares, tackling horrendous slopes, and turning his crawler in the very burn to do, as he sees it, the best and most complete job. Once the furrow has been turned, nobody can blame the planting gang if they plant every yard of it up to the ride, the fence, or the burn. The forester cannot be everywhere, and even in places where very precise plans have been made and agreed, ploughing and planting has gone ahead exactly as before. *The most careful briefing and supervision at all levels will be needed before intelligent forest design can become a reality.*

Small Woodlands

In miniature the same principles apply to the pheasant coverts and plantations of lowland Britain as to the sprawling northern conifer blocks. Clearly, everything has to be reduced in scale, but fallow, roe and muntjac exist in very large numbers throughout the country, and provision has to be made to control them efficiently, safely and humanely. Some deer will be shot as they feed in the fields, especially in the doe season but, in contrast to continental experience, roebucks in this country tend to disappear into the woods by late April or early May and remain there until the autumn. Unless there are openings inside, in the form of well-kept rides or special control clearings, collecting a trophy buck will be a matter of luck and chance.

Fortunately, the type of woodland management that benefits pheasants also suits roe deer, and the wide sunny rides recommended by the Game Conservancy for game coverts can be utilised for deer control.[24] Shrubs planted along the sides can be chosen as much to provide browse as for shelter and warmth for the birds. Naturally if deer are present any new planting has to be protected until it is established. After this, browsing will keep the bushes from becoming overgrown and draughty.

Even where no game interest exists, main rides should be made as wide as possible to allow them to dry out. A narrow, overgrown ride soon becomes a dank tunnel, and any traffic reduces it to a mud bath rivalling the battlefields of the Somme. A few broad, well-drained rides with woody browse at each side not only facilitate forestry and deer control operations, but encourage the growth of herbs enjoyed by a variety of butterflies. Birds such as the nightingale and the blackcap will nest in this low cover, and the dormouse, threatened through loss of habitat, will also benefit.

Frost pockets and other difficult sites for forestry are not restricted to the northern woods. Even if the area concerned is very small, it may be overlooked by a well-sited high seat at a convenient distance. Misplaced enthusiasm on the part of the forester for a 100 per cent stocking rate can lead to these places being repeatedly beaten up, sometimes for many years, until the surrounding crop is already tall. Far better to recognise the underlying factor which prevents the trees from growing and develop alternative uses, rather than throw good money after bad. One tiny frost hollow in Dorset which was less than 0.25 hectares ($\frac{1}{2}$ acre) in extent regularly yielded a Gold Medal roebuck, besides other quality trophies and many does. The return in fees and venison would have eclipsed any possible yield of timber even if it had been possible to grow good trees rather than stunted, frosted bushes.

A passion for tidy forestry has been responsible for destroying many woodland features important to conservation or deer control. Similarly, tidy farming has cleared away or filled up the odd field corners and damp spots beloved of wildlife. The gain in real terms is minimal, the loss is not yet fully realised.

8 *Clearings and Feeding Areas*

The proportion of plantable land set aside purely for deer control in a large block of commercial forestry should not normally exceed 2 per cent of the total. To this may be added land left open for other reasons, such as extraction and access roads, power lines, frost pockets and difficult sites which may be improved in one way or another to attract the deer. Burn-sides and gullies left unplanted in accordance with landscape policy or to protect the fishing also make their contribution without this sacrifice being set wholly against the needs of deer management.

Even so, any concession needs to be justified by a solid contribution to forest protection, or by an annual harvest of venison or trophies. Some capital cost and a reasonable amount of annual maintenance are likely to pay handsome dividends, not least because the stalker's time is spent more profitably sitting over a clearing which has been made into a magnet for deer, rather than one where they only appear occasionally or by chance.

As well as making deer control more efficient by creating clearings and additional food sources in the forest, consideration should be given to the possibility that less damage will be done to forest or farm crops as a result. What alternatives are available to the deer manager? In descending order of expense, they may be listed as follows:

Artificial feeding

Fodder crops

Grass

Trees and shrubs planted for browse

Improvement to existing ground vegetation

Improvement to existing browse

Artificial Feeding

In some European countries, forestry and deer management have become separated: an unhappy situation, fraught with problems. Neither side is likely to make concessions and both suffer. In the absence of natural food in the dark woods, any new plantations are subject to heavy damage, and have to be protected, either by fencing or deterrents. The deer manager is forced to resort to expensive hand feeding especially in areas where snow lies throughout a long winter. The number of feeding places which can be kept supplied has a practical limit, and only dominant males are likely to get much benefit. These pampered individuals hang about, not troubling to forage for themselves but making up their fibre requirements by tearing bark from neighbouring trees. Serious bark stripping is a normal feature of woods in the immediate vicinity of mangers and hay racks. Often, the object of providing quantities of extra fodder is to produce larger trophies or maintain a heavier stock of deer than the forest will support naturally.

With our relatively mild climate, and general agreement among deer managers that the population should be kept in balance with the natural food available, we should aim at habitat improvement, but stop short of hand feeding unless there are unusually good reasons for it.

Providing artificial food for deer does nevertheless have some practical applications. Fallow deer in the New Forest have always raided farm crops, to receive rough justice in return. Traffic accidents involving fallow bucks also became a problem in the post-war years. A deer sanctuary was established in the early sixties which soon attracted a large proportion of the local bucks. For most of the year they are held by regular feeding with potatoes. Raids on agricultural crops have been reduced as a result and fewer bucks are killed on the roads. Each September they disperse to traditional rutting stands, some quite far off, but they come back again a month or so later.

A similar position exists with the very heavy red deer which are to be found in Thetford Chase, in Norfolk. Carrots and other intensive crops are grown nearby, and the very existence of this isolated herd has been threatened by retaliatory shooting on the fields. Thanks to the formation of a local deer management society and the unselfishness of some of the landowners involved, a scheme was started of feeding the deer with waste carrots, thus keeping them within the forest and out of harm's way to some extent: a logical and appropriate solution.

The foodstuff to be provided must depend to a large extent on what is cheaply and readily available, but it also has to be palatable. Throwing out mouldy hay or rotten potatoes is no answer. The deer also need time to become accustomed to a change of diet. Animal lovers are often moved to take hay out to hard-pressed deer in very severe weather. Unless they have already had access to something of the sort their rumen flora, on which deer depend for the breakdown of cellulose, will be unable to cope and the animals can literally die of starvation with a full stomach. Adaptation may take up to a fortnight before a new feed can be fully digested. In emergency, cutting down ivy or conifer foliage (not yew) will benefit the deer immediately because it is similar to their normal diet. Concentrates, such as deer cobs, are fed in some places in the Highlands, but in woodlands this should not be warranted. Supplement blocks intended to improve the utilisation of poor fodder are taken freely by red and fallow, but a convincing case has yet to be made for them.

In very thick woodland, in which every sort of browse is abundant and where the stalker has few places where deer can be seen at all, some form of baiting may be needed in the interests of deer control. The idea may be repugnant, but might have to be considered as a stop-gap, especially in the case of muntjac.

Salt Licks
Once the taste has been acquired, deer will take salt freely, licking the run-off from posts and stumps on which salt blocks have been placed, and eating the impregnated earth beneath. It is assumed to have some tonic effect.

Natural rock salt is now difficult to obtain. Large manufactured blocks weighing about 10kg and containing various trace elements are the best alternative. They can be spiked to the top of a substantial post, or placed on large, flat-topped tree stumps. Rain will slowly dissolve the block, but even when it has gone deer, once hooked, will continue to visit the place.

To get them started, powdered salt can be mixed with mole-hill earth and placed on the stump. Tobacco is as habit-forming to deer as it is to man. A few cigarettes broken up into the mixture may get results.

Curiously enough, deer in the United Kingdom are more reluctant to take salt than is the case abroad. Possibly with a longer tradition of deer management on the Continent the habit has had many years to become established. Fallow are the first to use salt licks. Roe rarely touch them. On the whole, however, salt as an attractant is disappointing. Many enthusiasts have tried it, and – disillusioned – have given up the attempt.

Fodder Crops

Deer if they are hungry enough will eat almost anything, but something attractive is needed for specially-planted feed patches. The need for cultivations should be kept to a minimum, so either a simple crop like stubble turnips can be chosen, or a perennial such as artichokes which will have several years of useful life before needing to be re-sown. A list of suggestions is given in the Reference Section.

Fencing will almost certainly have to be considered to protect the crop while it is growing or to prevent it from being eaten up before the hungriest time of the year. Sheep and cattle will also have to be excluded if they share the area with the deer. Low netting is needed for one, a strand or two of barbed wire for the other. If the plot is intended to be used for a number of years, permanent fencing is justified. Otherwise the young crop can be safeguarded with electric fencing as suggested in Chapter 4.

As with other feed areas, several small plots are much better than one of several hectares. The deer will make fuller use of them, more can be shot without risk of scaring them off completely, and disturbance will be less.

From a control point of view, patches of feed are particularly valuable during the doe season. If they are established near woods which are difficult to stalk, either lacking paths, or possibly because of a safety factor, the proper complement of females can be taken when they come out to graze.

Some strips specially planted for pheasants can serve two purposes if the right crop is chosen,[25] but game crops such as mustard, canary grass, or maize will be frosted and beaten down by late January or February, the critical time for does. If kale is chosen, the most frost-hardy varieties are Bittern, Canson, Maris Kestrel, Proteor and Thousand Head.

Crops may be planted to keep deer away from the fields, with the object of protecting agriculture or the deer themselves from unwelcome harrassment. In planning the necessary cultivations one must remember that the 'magnet' crop must be more attractive to the deer than those in the fields, and so it has to receive a generous dose of fertiliser. Too often this expensive item is skimped, and the cultivations are hurriedly done when no other farm work is pressing. The result will not be fully effective.

Grass and Other Crops for Grazing

The needs of deer concerning grass crops are diametrically opposed to those of farm stock. Instead of a quick flush of lush growth in the spring, they prefer to graze on grass less than 10cm (4in) high. The same applies to cereal crops, which are sought out avidly until they reach this height, to be largely disregarded afterwards. Roe, in particular, need a high protein diet, and cannot digest large quantities of wet grass, as cows do. They can be seen on ploughed fields, seeking out the first shoots of couch grass (*Agropyron repens*) to re-grow, and appear to prefer them even when the new crop is through. Grazing on winter-sown crops has been shown to be less damaging than might be imagined, *and ceases immediately the field is sprayed.*

Turning these preferences to the requirements for a deer 'lawn', one needs grasses with a long growing season and a prostrate habit. The usual agricultural mixtures containing rygrass soon get ahead of the deer except where the grazing pressure is very severe. They will need topping at regular intervals unless a hay crop is taken for winter feeding. All this is very labour-intensive. Mixtures intended for sheep promise better, with fescues (*Festuca* spp.) and meadow grass (*Poa pratensis*) predominating. The inclusion of herbs such as yarrow (*Achillea millefolium*) or chickory (*Chichorium intybus*) and red or white clover (*Trifolium* spp.) will make the plot more attractive.

Fallow deer demonstrated a marked preference for Yorkshire fog (*Holcus lanatus*) in some trials in Wiltshire. Obtaining seed of this detested weed from agricultural merchants might be difficult, but small quantities can be harvested by hand. Various species of vetch are freely eaten by deer. The most commonly grown is Lucerne (*Medicago sativa*) but seed of some others is obtainable. Sarradella (*Ornithopus sativus*) will grow in very poor sandy soil in the south, and is said to be irresistible to deer.

Ground set aside for deer is rarely very rich. To keep the grass sweet and growing throughout the season, regular but light applications of fertiliser are needed. Depending on the underlying soil chemistry, slow-acting fertilisers, such as ground mineral phosphate or granular basic slag, have the best effect. Nitrogen tends to produce a quick, brief flush, and should be used with discretion.

Trees and Shrubs Planted for Browse

With men and machinery available, agriculturally based estates will find moments when the odd patch of fodder can be sown in strategic places. Without this help, the cheaper and long-term alternative of planting trees and shrubs as deer food can be chosen. This method of reducing damage has

already been mentioned in Chapter 3, 'Minimising Damage' and Chapter 5 'Planning Effective Deer Control'.

Many hardwoods make good deer browse (see list in Reference Section), but from the point of view of good management, the ideal is one which is easy to propagate, grows quickly in a wide variety of soil types and coppices readily. Nothing fills this specification better than the willow in all its varieties. A palatability trial some years ago gave top marks to the tea-leaf willow (*Salix phylicifolia*) but the difference is marginal. All are browsed freely and make excellent fraying stocks for every deer species. Most will root freely from cuttings, and when cut down they coppice well, sending up a mass of succulent shoots. Grey and goat willows, *Salix cinerea* and *Salix caprea*, are more difficult to strike, but do better on drier locations.

One willow species or another exists nearly everywhere, and a few experiments will show whether walking-stick sized cuttings will root when pressed into the ground, whether smaller twigs have to be rooted in the garden and then transplanted, or if they need to be put in a jar of water for a few weeks until the first roots have grown. In general, narrow-leaved osiers root most readily, the sallows need more sympathetic treatment. The best time for taking cuttings is in March.

Having discovered an easily-propagated species suitable to the locality, nothing could be easier than to take a bundle of cuttings each time the wood is visited, and thrust them in at suitable intervals. Transplants and the more slender twigs have to be protected from deer until they are established, even if this just takes the form of a twiggy branch laid over the top. If sticks of 1m or more long and 2cm ($\frac{3}{4}$in) in diameter can be persuaded to take root, they can be left to chance. A proportion of them should survive. Trees put in at the same time as the main crop will have a much better chance because there will not yet be enough cover to harbour deer.

In an attempt to add to the beauty and diversity of a big hill plantation in Inverness-shire, 10,000 hardwood whips, mostly rowan, were planted at the corners and along the rides. Sadly, all were eaten by mountain hares, roe and red deer. The owner argued that individual protection for such a large number of plants would have been prohibitively expensive. With hindsight it would have been better to buy fewer trees and spend the balance protecting them. At least this small number would have survived.

If browse plants have to be purchased, the choice should lie with those likely to do best for given soil and climate. Many will also beautify the landscape with flaming autumn foliage or clusters of berries which will be appreciated by the birds. Rowan grows well in a wide variety of soil types, and other possibilities are dogwood, spindle and whitebeam for the south and calcareous soils. Aspen, gean and bird cherry will withstand the northern winters, and broom is a good choice for sandy soils. Wherever possible, native species should be chosen for their value to conservation.

In the previous chapter the predilection which roe have for anything exotic or unusual was mentioned, and this should be exploited if a special clearing is to be planted up for them, even if it should pain the conservation purists. Ask a nurseryman at the end of his lifting season for reject transplants or almost any uncommon species which may have been left unsold, and plant them in straggling lines, as if a plantation had already failed. The roe will immediately feel at home there.

In deep peat, lodgepole pine may be the best choice to provide browse. It is very palatable, and will be taken in preference to Scots pine, or the spruces, which may constitute the main crop. In acid and hill situations the two native species, Rowan and Aspen (*Populus tremula*) may be chosen. Both are avidly eaten by deer.

Holly, in spite of its prickles, makes good browse, as any visitor to the New Forest can see. Gorse is also good when young, though it is too bad a forest weed to be recommended for planting. In Scotland, and on higher altitude plantings, heather is the main winter browse for all deer species. Birch is low on the preference list, but is eaten by deer in the north, probably for lack of any alternative.

Improvement to Existing Ground Vegetation

Here one is dealing with extremes – from the super-abundant second growth of the fertile soils of southern England to shifting, leached sands on which little will grow at all. In the vast northern forests, rides and other spaces available for improvement will be covered with heather or white grasses (*Molinia* or *Deschampsia* spp.). Once the canopy has been removed from a typical south-country hazel wood a mass of flowers, herbs and coppice growth springs up. Wood anemones and bluebells are followed by taller plants: woodspurge, hemp agrimony, thistles and burdock. In the second year the hazel re-growth will be high enough to hide a roe.

While the ancient practice of coppice-with-standards persisted, small parcels of each wood were cut in rotation, making a perfect habitat for many birds, flowers and butterflies, and abundant feeding for deer. Nowadays the conversion of many traditional coppices to high forest, conifer or hardwood, means that cutting is no longer on a short rotation. The margins of wide rides often form the last reservoir of many woodland species. Management of these plant communities now has a highly important ecological significance, and provides in addition a valuable source of deer browse.

Given a ride which is wide enough to admit the sunlight, a central access path should be mown every year to encourage a good grass turf, pleasant to walk on and resistant to a reasonable amount of wheeled traffic. On either side is a strip cut as high as the scrub cutter will allow, ideally 20–30cm (8–12in). Cutting is only done in alternate winters to allow many insect food plants to seed, and to provide habitat for a wide variety of wildlife. Cutting in the second year prevents it from becoming a jungle and the ride overgrown. Taller bushes can be left on the edge of the high trees.

In bracken areas, making deer clearings to last all summer can be a problem. Either the largest proportion of roebucks should be taken before the bracken hides them early in June, or the weed can be treated with Asulox. Some regrowth and gradual recolonisation is to be expected, and further applications of the chemical will be needed.

On acid and leached sands the only possible improvement to the ground vegetation is by repeated applications of fertiliser to a basically unpalatable sward. What beneficial effect there is soon disappears and these problem areas are most economically tackled by planting shrubs such as broom, rather than becoming committed to an endless and costly maintenance programme.

Heather in itself is a very valuable food resource to deer, yielding as it does fairly high quality browse most of the year. The traditional method of management by burning is probably out of the question in a forest environment, though odd patches may be renewed in this way. Otherwise, the tractor and scrub cutter will have to be employed to take off old woody growth and encourage new shoots. Draining, which may be needed as a normal part of ride maintenance, also has a beneficial effect on heather.

White grass hills, such as are found in the wetter parts of the north of England and Scotland indicate an impoverished soil. In some places heather has been eliminated by over-grazing or over-burning. The rank, matted vegetation has a short growing season, soon yellowing and dying back. Deer if they are hungry will graze it while it stays green, but disregard it later. The technique developed at Eskdalemuir is to cut down through the mat with a chain-type cutter to expose the roots. Regrowth is sought out even by roe deer. Fertiliser has also some effect, though short-lived. If pockets of mineral soil occur in a peat area, these places will respond best to any effort to improve the feeding.

Improvement to Existing Browse

Potential browse can be found in almost every open space in established woodland, even if it is not immediately obvious. A search may well discover small bushes which have been suppressed by the canopy, or by heavy browsing. Large willow, rowan or whitethorn trees may be coppiced to produce a lavish crop of new growth. Scrub oak, overgrown hazel or aspen can receive the same treatment. Anything which is already established is a double bonus compared to the laborious and slow business of planting and protecting new trees or shrubs.

The question is often one of degree: how much to cut to give the deer plenty on which to feed without making so open a clearing that they will be afraid to visit it in daylight, or how to control the second growth so that one year's clearing does not turn into next year's impenetrable thicket. A coppice area cut out of woodland should have enough overhead shade left to limit the growth of bramble, itself the ideal browse. Some cut stumps may have to be treated with herbicide to keep alleyways clear and limit the annual task of cutting coppice re-growth. If the clearing is used by deer a great deal, they will do most of this work themselves, but a few trees will always get away from them and need trimming.

Willows are often found growing in the frost pockets and boggy areas which are most easily set aside for deer control. The upper branches of an established tree are out of browsing height and the stem will be too big to act as a roe fraying stock. A minute's work with a saw is all that is needed, and the twigs can either be taken for cuttings, or left for the deer. Juniper is left untouched until late in the winter, and for this reason is extremely valuable in harsh climates, but will not grow again when cut, and any bushes should be left alone.

9 Versatility in Stalking Techniques

Still Hunting

In attempting to find deer without their becoming alarmed, the stalker has to learn a very specialised technique founded on acute observation coupled with intimate knowledge of the habits of that particular species. Training the eye not to rove quickly round the scene is the first stage. Patience is

essential, and confidence to assume that there is enough of a chance of a deer being there to make a minute examination of each vista worthwhile. Nothing is worse than hurrying from place to place. Once in the wood, you are just as likely to see a deer where you are as anywhere else, in fact more likely.

Look carefully now all around as far as you can see. *But do not look for a deer.* Remember this singular advice. Do not forget it for a moment. One of the greatest troubles that besets the beginner is looking all the time *for a deer*. If the artist's deer is in sight you will see him quickly enough. Never mind that beast at all. Spend all your time in looking for *spots* and *patches* of light grey, dark grey, brown, or even black. Examine all you can see from only the size of your hand to the size of a small goat. Never mind the shape of them. Examine, too, everything that looks like the thick part of a thicket, and every blur or indistinct outline in a brush. No matter how much it may look like a bit of stump, fallen log, shade, or tangle of brush, or how little it may in shape resemble a deer; if it is in brush, or anywhere where you cannot see clearly what it is, give it a second, even a third, look. Look *low*, too, *very low*, along the ground. And be very careful how you run your eye over a bit of brush, deciding that it is *too low* for a deer to be in without your seeing him. Not only does a deer in the woods generally look entirely unlike the deer that stands in Imagination's park, but it *does not stand half so high in the woods* as it does in that park. When un-suspicious, a deer often has his head down, and this, too, makes him still lower. You need not be looking at this time of day for a deer lying down, but look *just as low* along the ground as if you were looking for one lying down.

So wrote Theodore Van Dyke in *The Still Hunter*.[26] His advice is just as valid for Britain now as it was for the United States at the turn of the century.

We are concerned here with polishing, varying and adapting this technique to produce the maximum return from the stalker's time and effort. Blind adherence to any rule, no matter how sound, will not be as effective as intelligent use of the knowledge and understanding of deer behaviour which can be built up over the years and adapted to one locality. Besides anything else, deer are very adaptable animals, capable of adjusting their behaviour not only to the normal changes of season, food supply or weather in order to live successfully in divergent habitats, but also to avoid contact with man by reacting to human activity patterns. Because of our habit of wasting the summer mornings by staying in bed, woodland deer have adopted a crepuscular habit to some extent, emerging to feed at dusk and dawn. This is not, however, their natural rhythm[27] but an adaptation which can as easily change in response to regular disturbance. For a couple of decades or more the sport of woodland stalking has been rapidly gaining in popularity. Some stalkers have found recently that there is less activity at first light, but a surprising amount in the late morning. Weather also affects movement, and therefore stalking success. On cold mornings in summer or winter, the deer may not stir until the sun is up, and then only in places where they can enjoy the first warmth. It is delightful to watch fallow does indulging in apparently aimless romps with their fawns just at sunrise, which can be assumed to be warming up exercises. Dew-fall in dry weather often marks the start of activity at dusk, for wild deer drink but rarely.[28] Around each full moon fewer are to be seen by day, presumably because they take advantage of moonlit nights to move and feed in safety.

This is not to suggest that the stalker should abandon the early mornings. Indeed these are his bread and butter. Some who have been brought up in the skills of hill stalking do not take easily to the necessity of early rising. Equally, visitors from the Continent who go stalking red deer in Scotland for the first time are staggered at the thought of going out after breakfast, rather than being at the top of the mountain before dawn. Their tradition is based on woodland stalking and we still have much to learn about it from them.

If one assumes that deer study humankind as if their lives depended on it (as is indeed the case) it is easier to avoid falling into a pattern of stalking which they will soon recognise. The larger the block of forest, the easier to vary routes, times and the actual ground covered or disturbed. Small areas can easily be over-stalked and the deer made wary or nocturnal.

No matter how careful the stalker is to work up-wind, he leaves a broad wash of scent behind and downwind of his route, so by the time he reaches the other end of the wood, virtually every deer will be aware that danger has been present. Repeating the same manoeuvre at the same time next day will find them already alert, by the third, few will show themselves. They must also be assumed to discriminate between the scent and behaviour of the stalker, and of other passers-by such as woodmen, picnic parties and so on who are quickly recognised as harmless. Forest workers often comment on how tame the deer are, and how numerous! – mostly to the forester.

One of the commonest mistakes made by beginners in the first flush of enthusiasm is to attempt to trace the movement patterns of deer by creeping laboriously along their racks or paths. This not only has the effect of terrifying the local deer, but is labour in vain, because deer paths have an infuriating habit of petering out. Far better to walk noisily through the undergrowth on some sort of grid system, and note the bedding areas, tracks, droppings and other evidence of occupation for transfer to a large-scale map. In the case of the larger deer species, the main road crossing points, racks through hedges, soiling pits, scrapes, fraying stocks and feeding areas when plotted on a map will be revealing in their evidence of regular movement patterns. Roe territories can also be roughly defined, and this work will be more valuable than time-consuming attempts at census-taking.

The biggest problem we face in understanding and outwitting deer is the fact that while their sight is not exceptional and we can comprehend their hearing, acute though it is, they live in a world of scent which is lost to us. We can, however, observe domestic animals and draw conclusions and parallels from their behaviour. For example, weather affects cattle in much the same way as deer, and a careful look in the fields en route for an early-morning stalking expedition can give a good forecast of what the deer can be expected to be doing. Are the cows up and feeding, or lying down chewing the cud? Are they huddled in the lee of the hedges? In the latter case most deer will also be in sheltered places. The list can be extended, always remembering that the rut breaks most established rules.

Use of the Stick

Any aid to straight shooting is worth testing in the widely differing conditions under which woodland deer are pursued. Of the many options open to the stalker, perhaps the most useful is the stalking stick although it will definitely need quite a bit of conscious adaptation on the part of the stalker before he begins to appreciate the benefits. In open country a short stick about 2.25m (4ft) long is ideal, steadying the stalker on rough ground, acting as a brake downhill, and serving as a support for the rifle for a kneeling or sitting shot. Even when shooting prone the stick may be used to give extra elevation over rank vegetation or uphill which would be awkward and uncertain without assistance. It is either stuck into the ground or laid at an angle against a tree or stone.

In the woods a prone shot is rare, and often deer are encountered at such short range that no movement is possible beyond the essential raising and lowering of the binoculars preparatory to getting the rifle up and steady. Standing shooting is the rule in thick cover, and there is unlikely to be a tree just at the right place from which to shoot. Three paces to the nearest may be out of the question with a suspicious buck at seventy yards. In young woodlands nothing may be thick enough to give a firm support. In those conditions a stout stick reaching up to the stalker's forehead is required. Using it he can stand up and take reasonable shots with confidence, though practice is needed. A right-handed shot must accustom himself to stalking with the stick in his left hand, and the rifle, muzzle down, over his right shoulder. Only thus can he get a shot off with the minimum of movement. The stick need not have a fork at the top, because it will be grasped by three fingers of the left hand at whatever height is convenient, thumb and first finger forming a rest for the rifle. Straight, seasoned hazel is ideal, being light and strong. For a tall man, about 1.83m (6ft) is best, and the end can be protected with a rubber ferrule. Some stalkers favour a steel spike, which can be thrust into the ground, but this tends to clink on stones.

A bipod attached to the rifle fore-end is highly efficient where many shots are taken prone. A long-leg model is available which can be used sitting.

Moving Deer

Rifle shooting is accepted as the most humane form of deer control, but claims are made that stalking cannot control the increase of some species, notably roe. This has proved true in some situations, especially in very large areas of blanket-planted conifers, and in areas where the demand for stalking is insufficient, or where amateur assistance in deer culling is actively discouraged for one reason or another.

If foresters are expected to make the concessions to the layout of their plantations that have been suggested in order to facilitate deer control, deer stalkers must reciprocate by developing and making use of every humane control method necessary to produce a harmonious balance between forestry and deer.

The greatest problem facing the deer manager operating on a large scale is to kill sufficient females during the legal season in winter. Days are short, the weather uncertain, and the woods may be disturbed by pheasant shooting or fox hunting as well as normal forest work. As a result, few stalkers are in the happy position of having accounted for the full tally of female deer by the end of the season. If this is repeated year after year as is often the case, the deer population not only becomes unbalanced, but its productivity gets out of hand.

This situation must be avoided at all costs if humane control is to continue. The moving of does to concealed rifles is a legitimate way to supplement traditional still hunting, and despite the understandable reluctance on the part of most riflemen to fire at moving targets, proper training and careful planning of moves can produce very useful results without materially increasing the risk of losing wounded deer.

The requirements are that the rifleman should be trained, and that the deer should be stationary, or moving only slowly. Most game shots visit the shooting school and practise on clay pigeons not only when they are learning, but before each season. In Sweden, where very large numbers of deer have to be shot every year, a network of shooting ranges has been built up where deer hunters can get experience of shooting at moving targets.[29] A very high standard is expected on the range, and stalkers who measure up to it are well equipped to shoot accurately when a deer comes past them in the forest. While shooting tests on the Swedish pattern are still regarded with some suspicion here, we have always taken pride in displaying the highest standards of marksmanship and consideration for our quarry. Moving has to have a place in our deer management, and now is the time for training facilities to be created, first for professional stalkers, and soon after for part-timers who have problems in achieving their culling targets. Otherwise the evils of shooting out of season and at night, the use of the shotgun and eventually even poison will be imposed as disagreeable but necessary alternatives.

The difference between moving and driving needs to be defined, because one is basically acceptable, the other not. In essence, moving involves a small number of rifles assisted by one or two movers, and possibly a dog to dislodge the deer, but not to chase them. The deer are induced to move along their accustomed paths without any panic. They are ambushed by the rifles at places where they are already pausing to look back and can thus be identified and a careful shot taken. In contrast, driving involves a large party of rifles and beaters who frighten the deer enough to make them run at speed past the shooters. Little possibility is offered to distinguish the sex or to assess the beast before shooting, and the chances of wounding are much increased.

The best situation for moving is where small woods are interspersed with fields, or in the long narrow woods which are often found along the contours of an escarpment. Escape routes will soon be learned. The rifle does not wait where the deer break cover, which they can be expected to do at speed having been disturbed, but at the edge of the next piece of cover to which they are making. They will have slowed down by then, and may well stop and look back before vanishing into the thicket. Suitably placed high seats may be needed for safety on flat ground. In larger blocks of woodland the deer are likely to stop before crossing a ride, and then gallop over which makes for difficult shooting unless points are chosen where cover is either low or thin at the ride sides so that they can be seen and shot there.

At Eskdalemuir the technique used is to blank-in one block, in pheasant shooting parlance, nothing being shot in this preliminary manoeuvre. The object is to send disturbed deer into the block which is really intended to be moved. This puts the residents on foot. High seats are then manned on crossing points and two dogs with bells on their collars with two dog handlers move gently through this block, upwind so that the dogs can wind the deer. The majority of does are shot coming back into the block which was blanked-in. Roe are the quarry in this forest. They are more difficult to get to move far than red or fallow deer, so relatively small areas should be taken in.

With the larger deer a variant of this small-scale move can also be productive. This is to man as many high seats as possible in an area. Getting stalkers to their places may be enough to put deer on the move, and shots here and there will keep them circulating. A man may be needed to help the process, but he must know the ground well enough to keep out of the firing line.

If the forest has been laid out properly, there will be a number of open feeding areas commanded by seats. These can be manned by a team of stalkers from dawn one day. As they are disturbed at one place, the deer will probably make for another.

No moves or manoeuvres involving general disturbance can be repeated more than once or twice in a season. The deer soon get wise. There is great merit in co-operation between stalkers, because of the returns from various types of move and from the companionship and exchange of ideas which refresh men in a lonely job.

Another form of collaboration between stalkers is for two men to 'still hunt' in the traditional way, but in adjacent blocks. Deer disturbed by the one may well show up in front of the other. This works best on rather open ground, and it need not be said that both men must know the ground well so that neither strays into the other's territory, nor shoots towards him.

Kenneth Macarthur, pioneer of enlightened deer management in southern Scotland, uses a technique for the small woods of his part of the country which is a combination of stalking and moving. In his correspondence he writes:

My method is for the mover to still hunt towards the ambush point. [He gets a surprising number of chances.] The ambushing rifle knows the 'break points' and 'entry points'. As well as using the entry points as described, I like to wait in the wood 50–100m before the break-point where I can see the main run. High seats are an aid as a shot from the sky confuses a bunch of deer. The mover does not act like a beater, but like a hunter.

In addition to moving does in the winter, the wiliest roebuck can sometimes be outwitted by a well thought-out move. Red deer in plantations can often be moved round the fence, and the bachelor parties of red, fallow and sika males which are often such a nuisance in farm land are vulnerable as well, once their behaviour has been observed.

Calling

The concept of luring a love-sick male by playing on his susceptibilities is repugnant to some people, savouring of unsporting behaviour. Two facts should be considered: firstly, the technique is difficult to master, needing considerable understanding of deer behaviour and psychology. Secondly, it may be the only way to get one particular animal to show himself in thick forest. Calling is perfectly legitimate, provided that it is used within the management plan, and not as a means of over-exploiting the deer population.

Practically all our knowledge has come from the Continent, where the art of calling and the excitement inseparable from it make the roe and stag rut peak times in the sporting year. The calling of roe has been attempted here for many years, in fact one of the best English heads at the 1954 Dusseldorf Exhibition was a buck shot by Frank Sykes in Great Ridge Wood in response to a call as long ago as 1939. Red deer on the open hill in Scotland are vulnerable enough when they are rutting to make calling unnecessaary, but in the dense forests they now inhabit the position is entirely different. As deer control in this new environment is developed, calling will have to be taught and take its place as a necessary string to the woodland stalker's bow.

Sika calling has been developed virtually by the efforts of one man, Eric Masters of the Forestry Commission at Wareham in Dorset. His technique is now used successfully in many places where sika exist. Fallow, in contrast, do not respond well, although a rutting buck can be persuaded to move across his stand in response to a well-judged groan and thus reveal himself to the rifleman.

Red deer
Woodland stags do not roar as freely as their cousins on the heather. In fact, an old stag rarely consents to express himself with more than a deep grunt occasionally, while younger stags can only be expected to set up a chorus when clear frosty nights put an edge on their appetites. Even then, roaring will not usually continue long after dawn. This arises because of the different behaviour of red deer in woodland, where they normally live in small groups consisting of a stag and half a dozen or so hinds. Competition between stags, though undoubtedly present, is not so obtrusive as on the hill, and because

of the restricted visibility in the trees, groups can wander near one another without conflict.

Calling therefore is a very circumspect affair, imitating the stag's roar with a variety of tubular objects from lamp glasses to triton shells, as well as proprietory designs. Promiscuous calling in the hope of a reply is rarely successful. One hopes to hear a stag and reply to his roar, hoping that he will respond to the challenge and come to investigate. If two stalkers are out in roughly the same area they should beware of calling one another! Even the genuine article responding to a call will be in a highly charged emotional state, and in poor light may mistake the stalker for another stag. In case he is not shootable, it is advisable to have a tree handy.

Records and tape cassettes are available to demonstrate the right noises to make, but they are far better demonstrated by an expert, who will also be able to point out the likeliest spots.

Calling is only effective during the height of the rut, which varies from year to year, but can be expected from late September to the end of October.

Sika

The sika stag makes an unearthly triple whistle to demonstrate his presence. Hinds will either come to his rutting stand or, eternally feminine, visit his rival. His concern is thus to eject rivals and younger stags, and, like the red stag, he will answer a suitable whistle and come to see the intruder off.

Surprisingly, the best whistles for the purpose come out of children's squeaky rubber toys, but a number have to be pressed sharply before one with the right pitch can be found. Once selected, the squeaker unit is taken out and, to produce a life-like imitation of the sika stag's whistle, the squeaker is blown into the cupped hands, which are used to regulate the sound.

A stag responding to what he takes to be a rival can be persuaded to come briefly into the open, but will not go far from his rutting stand. The main advantage is that by doing so he sometimes steps outside the protective ring of young males who would otherwise alert him to the stalker's presence. Sika usually start whistling in the last few days of September, but the peak of rutting activity is slightly later than with red deer, and calling continues well into November.

Roe deer

In contrast to the larger deer, roe calling is based on various noises made by the doe, rather than stimulating the buck by imitations of a challenge by another male.

A doe coming into season will seek out a buck, squeaking to attract his attention, and encourage him to keep close company. Does are not averse to accepting service from another buck, but appear to resent any attempt on the part of the chosen consort to wander off or philander. Fawns are usually hidden during rutting play. Calling technique is based on these facts.

The easiest buck to call is an unattached wanderer, or a territorial buck temporarily without an in-season doe. If the conditions are right, he will come some distance to investigate the squeak of a doe, which is a piping call very similar to that made by young sparrow hawks. Most proprietory roe calls are made to imitate this noise which is commonly written as 'fiep'. A buck already in company of a doe will be difficult to detach, but the doe may herself respond to a fawn call (similar but higher pitched than the 'fiep') and bring the buck with her. Alternatively the stalker can use the distress call which is made by a young doe when pressed hard by a pursuing buck. This is a two-tone call ('pee-you') given at first softly and then increasingly loud.

While the music of calling is important, choice of time and place is vital. Calling is rarely successful before 15 July or after 20 August. The best days are hot and thundery; the best time between 8.00 a.m. and 2.00 p.m. Cold, wet or windy days are hopeless for calling. Bucks can be called from thicket into more open woodland, or back from the fields towards the woods, but they cannot be expected to face the open, though on some days they seem to go mad with the rut and throw away all caution. If a roe ring (a circular tramped path) is discovered, calling in the vicinity is often worth while.

Dogs

In the days of the old black-powder rifles, stalking parties on the hill were often accompanied by a dog to find or bay a wounded deer. The practice died out, though a well-trained dog will both wind unseen deer, and find a shot beast quickly, even if it is lying invisible in a peat hag. If they are useful on open ground, how much more does a stalker need the help of a dog in thick woodland. Even with a mortal shot, the deer may plunge off into heavy cover which may be the head-high bracken of mid-summer, or a 20-year old sitka plantation concealing the remains of deep forestry ploughing. In either case the deer may be lying dead within a few yards, and yet may never be found without the aid of a dog, or only when the venison is spoiled. In the unhappy event of a deer being wounded, the stalker's unaided efforts are unlikely to be successful. It is the moral duty of every stalker to own and train a deer dog if he possibly can, in the interests of humanity as well as the game account.

Gundogs, such as the labrador, can be trained for the work without prejudice to their abilities in the shooting field. They have the advantage of walking to heel, and therefore being on the spot when needed. Breeds of a more excitable nature have to be left behind, to be fetched from the car or from the kennel. It must be admitted that the small continental breeds of bloodhound such as the Styrian or Hanoverian have far superior noses for following a stale line to anything we have in this country, nor is the science of training as well developed here. Even so, a dog used to the work will find many deer, and save time, venison and distress. Some can be taught to bark when they find; some do so naturally. Otherwise a collar and bell must be carried so that the dog's whereabouts can be judged as he works in thick cover. Hound breeds can be taught to follow directly on a line, while a gundog ranges downwind of it. A slow hound such as a dachshund can be worked on a long leash.

In addition to finding shot game, dogs are extremely useful for pointing deer if they are at heel, and for use in moving them to concealed rifles. For the latter, hound breeds are better avoided. They will stick to a line even when the line of rifles has been passed, and may be difficult to find or catch; a most frustrating and time-wasting affair. Curiously enough, the setter makes a good dog for moving. Their bird-dog nature and training is to range at a distance from the handler, but not to hunt a line. Deer are thus put on foot, but not harried. Many stalkers use small terriers, in fact any dog with a nose can be trained to deer and one of small size can be taken up into a high seat. They are also slow, which is an advantage in every way, except in the event of a hunt after a deer with one leg broken, when speed is of the essence.

One caution should be borne in mind when using dogs for moving. The disturbance resulting from one day's efforts (or for that matter from foxhounds drawing a covert) can be forgotten. If it is repeated over the course of some days the deer will move away or materially alter their habits. In a wood in Wiltshire moving does with dogs for several days in February had the effect of dislodging four territorial bucks to such permanent effect that they had not returned the following May. Their places had been taken

by a number of yearlings. Nothing can be more disastrous to a herd of deer than constant harrassment by loose dogs.

If there is one field in which we have much to learn, it is in dog training for deer work. There is a great need for enthusiasts who will give the same to this branch of dog work as it is such a feature of the field trial movement. Very few dogs in the U.K. would measure up to the continental standard of following a trail of blood 40 hours old for 1200m. Amateurs' dogs are unlikely to get enough practice, so artificial trails are necessary, otherwise they give up too soon. A lead is desirable to force the dog to go slowly and concentrate.

In very thick cover a lead is useless, and the dog must work loose, with a bell, and 'bark dead' when he finds. When training a dog to deer, he should be encouraged to find, return to the handler and then go back again to the deer to show the way. As in all things, the stalker must consider the gamekeeper and work with him. The keeper will not object to the use of a steady dog, or even to some disturbance in order to retrieve a wounded deer. Anything beyond this, especially the use of dogs for moving deer, should be done with his approval, and outside the peak of the pheasant season.

10 *Equipment for the Stalker*

A poorly-equipped stalker wastes time and opportunities, yet in comparison to the value of deer he brings in, the cost of proper tackle is very small. The stalker's work is by no means over when the deer is dead, and this chapter also considers methods of extracting and handling the carcase and basic preparation of trophies.

The Rifle

Choice of weapon

Shotguns are now illegal for deer shooting in England and Wales except under special circumstances, and rifles must have a minimum calibre of 6mm (.240in) with an expanding bullet giving a muzzle energy of more than 1700ft/lb. This not only eliminates all .22 rifles, but many obsolete types of larger calibre but low power. Scottish law still permits the use of .22 centrefire cartridges such as the .222 Remington and .22/250, both of which make good rifles for roe in careful hands. It is possible in future that the Scottish Law will be followed in England and Wales to allow the use of these potent .22 Centrefires for roe and muntjac (*see* Reference Section). For larger deer, or where an all-round rifle is needed, a calibre should be selected which is potentially accurate, freely available and for which a variety of bullet weights are loaded commercially. The majority of stalkers use one of the following:

Calibre	Bullet weights grains	Muzzle velocity ft/sec	Muzzle energy ft/lb
.243 Winchester	80	3420	2077
	100	2960	1945
.270 Winchester	100	3480	2689
	130	3110	2791
	150	2900	2801
.30/'06	110	3380	1827
	130	3280	3108
	150	2920	2820
	180	2700	2913
	220	2410	2837
.308 Winchester	110	3280	1588
	125	3100	2538
	150	2820	2627
	180	2620	2648
	200	2450	2743
.275 (7 × 57mm)	150	2756	2530
	175	2470	2370

Choosing the right bullet is vitally important to ensure clean, humane kills. A compromise has to be struck between expansion and penetration.

Lightly constructed bullets tend to break up too soon, creating surface wounds which may not be immediately fatal. Slow-expanding types designed for larger animals than deer may pass through the body without transferring their energy to the surrounding tissues. On the whole, the lighter weight bullets in any calibre tend also to be more lightly constructed. For example, the 110 grain bullet for the .30/'06 cartridge is so fragile it is only suited to targets up to the size of a fox. The 130 grain is good for roe but can lack penetration on red deer, for which the 150 and 180 grain loads are better suited. At the top end is the 220 grain, designed for animals such as heavy antelopes, which will hardly expand on any of our deer unless a bone is struck. Despite this, great variation in performance can be found between similar loads from different manufacturers. Each stalker should be allowed to experiment, and choose a load in which he has confidence. Due regard should also be given to the type of country. If the woods are intersected by roads or invaded by the public, it is prudent to choose a fast, light-weight bullet which will break up on hitting a twig. Large bullets at comparatively low speeds will plough through a good deal of cover, and like the ordinary .22 rimfire, can ricochet alarmingly. The worst offender in this respect is the still-legal rifled slug fired from a 12 bore gun. High speed and fast expansion are potent safety factors, contrary to ill-informed opinion.

From the foregoing it should be clear that heavier bullets do less damage to the meat than lighter types. A heavy bullet in fact is less likely to do damage, and in consequence does not have a quick knock-down effect. This is not significant on open ground, but is vitally important in thick woodland. In addition, it may hit the deer but still retain enough speed and mass to constitute a danger on the other side.

The rifle itself does not need to be a de luxe model, but certain features are essential. The barrel must be accurate, the trigger pull unvarying, quite without drag and preferably adjustable for weight of pull. The action should be slick with a positive, silent and easily operated safety catch. The woodwork should not be liable to warp and so alter the rifle's zero. Most right-handed stalkers use bolt action magazine rifles. There is a definite advantage in having a quick second shot available, to finish off a wounded beast before it moves, or to take another out of the group. A wide choice is available, from plain but very serviceable weapons upwards. The advice of a gunsmith specialising in stalking rifles is the best guide, though there is a lot to be said for just seeing what your local professional uses to kill his deer.

Old rifles will probably have lost their accuracy, even if cartridges are still available. Non-corrosive ammunition did not come into universal use until fairly recently, and a second-hand rifle may well have been neglected sufficiently to ruin the bore. With reasonable care and maintenance and modern ammunition, barrel life should nowadays exceed 3000 rounds without great loss of accuracy, so it pays to buy new, or at least search for a rifle with a brief and known history.

Continental stalkers often use the double or set-trigger which allows the rifle to be fired with a feather-light touch on the trigger. In unpractised hands they can be extremely dangerous, and professional stalkers in this country have learned to be especially vigilant when a guest brings one along. They are at their best for deliberate shots from a high seat. For stalking conditions over here, a well-designed single-stage trigger with a crisp let-off around 1.2–1.3kg (2¾ to 3lb) will do a better job.

Sights

Telescopic sights are essential for woodland stalking, which takes place mostly at dawn and dusk. A good instrument will allow stalking to start earlier and continue later than is possible with iron sights, stretching the day by half an hour or more at each end, at just the times when deer are most likely to be on the move. The clear image and superimposed aiming mark (graticule or reticule) makes precise shooting possible to the full capacity of rifle and stalker. Humane kills and a minimum of wasted venison are the result.

A first-class scope is the best possible investment although it will cost as much again as a plain rifle. The choice is very wide, even disregarding cheap models designed for .22 rifles. Usually you get what you pay for and these qualities are brilliance and resolving power, precise internal adjustments and, above all, better reliability. A scope that changes zero between shots, or lets water in is virtually useless. Some have variable magnification, which increases the price and also the complexity of an instrument which has to stand up to the repeated hammer-blows of recoil as well as the rough-and-tumble of everyday use. A fixed four-power scope has less to go wrong, and is a good compromise for general use. A very low power is useful for shooting at moving deer. When the latter are at close range, which they should be, iron sights are the best for those with normal eyesight.

The graticule has to be a compromise between providing an aiming mark which does not obscure the target, and being so fine that it is difficult to see in the dusk. Various alternatives are offered, including cross-wires and dots, both of which are too indistinct for poor light, vertical and horizontal posts, or combinations of posts and cross-wires. If a post is chosen, it should be flat-topped, not pointed, otherwise the rifle will tend to shoot progressively higher as the light fails. Probably the best has four posts for easy visibility, with a small cross-hair joining them for accurate aim.

Iron sights may be retained on a scope-sighted rifle as a back-up in case of fogging or for close-range shots on moved deer, but mounting the scope high enough to be able to look through the iron sights below is inadvisable. The head has to be craned uncomfortably to look through the scope and there is a great risk of canting the rifle, which will make it shoot inaccurately.

Telescopic sights should be used to aid accurate shooting, not to indulge in shooting at over-long ranges.

Tuning and Zeroing

Possession of a good rifle and scope sight does not necessarily mean that each bullet will strike where intended, or that it will continue consistently to be accurate, even when properly adjusted. The cheaper the grade of rifle, the less hand finishing the manufacturer can put into it and the more supplementary work will be needed to get good results.

Three elements in consistent shooting deserve special attention: (*a*) the trigger pull, (*b*) the bedding of the barrel and action and (*c*) the tightness of all screws.

(a)   A heavy, or creepy pull is fatal to accuracy. Some stalkers with military training behind them like a two-stage pull, in which some movement of the trigger has to be taken up before a slightly heavier pressure actually fires the rifle. The majority, however, insist on a single pull with no lost motion whatever. In either case the let-off must be crisp, like breaking glass. The weight of the let-off should be light within the dictates of safety, and as stalkers' hands vary in sensitivity, some may favour as light a pull as 1kg (2.2lb) while others will choose one twice as heavy. Whatever the weight chosen, it must not change through wear or poor design. Standing shots, which are commonplace in woodland stalking, are particularly difficult with a heavy pull.

Most modern actions are adjustable for weight of let-off, creep and backlash (lost movement after firing). The action has to be removed from the woodwork to make adjustments, and as other matters have to be attended to in sequence before zeroing, the trigger can be adjusted first, or, in the case of a new weapon, after thorough removal of storage grease. Needless to say, a set of gunmaker's screwdrivers properly ground to fit each screw head is essential. Ordinary carpenter's tools will burr the slots. Two screws normally attach the metal parts to the stock, one at the tang behind the trigger guard, and one at the recoil stop below the chamber.

When adjusting the trigger pull, great care must be taken not to reduce the weight by partially disengaging the sear and bent (the firing mechanism), or by unskilled dressing of the sliding surfaces. This can produce an extremely dangerous situation where the rifle can be jarred off. Certain lubricants, especially those containing Molybdenum Disulphide can also reduce the pull-off. When in doubt, consult a competent gunsmith. Some actions are incapable of adjustment below 1.5kg (3½lb) without risk. Others can safely be taken down to 1kg (2.2lb). Set triggers have already been mentioned. They offer few advantages over a well-adjusted, crisp, single trigger, and in less than expert hands can be really dangerous. Most rifles fitted with them can be converted.

(b)   The barrel vibrations caused by firing the cartridge affect the bullet's path. If they are the same each time, accuracy will be enhanced. If they vary materially from shot to shot, accuracy will suffer. These vibrations are dampened by the wood of the fore-end if this touches the barrel, so any change in contact will affect the rifle's accuracy. A small amount of warping in damp weather can produce miss after miss. In attempts to counter this, rifles have been stocked with free-floating barrels in which there is no contact at all with the stock, with contact only at the fore-end tip, and with epoxy resin bedding of the whole barrel length, or just beneath the action.

Whatever method is adopted, it must be consistent. A full-floating or tip-contact rifle should be checked by sliding a slip of paper up and down to ensure that the clearance between barrel and stock is sufficient. Any

1   Rutting red deer

2   A fallow buck showing typical palmate antlers and long tail. Fallow come in a variety of colours and this buck is in winter coat. Light coloured underparts indicate that it would be chestnut with spots (common coloured) during the summer

3 A sika stag. Note the white marks on his forehead and below the hock. This stag has a six point head against the eight normally shown by a mature stag

4 A roe buck in summer coat. Their rich unspotted chestnut colour changes to a thick dark brown coat in October with prominent white tail patch (target)

5   A muntjac buck. Note the hunched pig-like silhouette, the forehead ridges which are prolonged into long furry pedicles, short tushes in the upper jaw and prominent sub-orbital glands below the eyes

6   Hurdle making. The coppice-with-standards regime which has now largely disappeared provided an ideal habitat for deer as well as for many other wildlife species

7 Large-scale afforestation. Large-scale forestry schemes like this need to be carefully planned if the future needs of deer control, landscape and amenity are to be built in. A steep area left unplanted in the middle distance will make an attractive break in the canopy when the forest eventually grows up

8 Ploughing moorland for afforestation. When the forest design plan has been established it is essential that the tractor driver himself is fully briefed and understands the reasons for leaving any areas unploughed otherwise he cannot be blamed for tackling as much of the ground as he dares, regardless of long-term needs

9 Typical roe deer browsing damage to Norway spruce. Eventually a leading shoot may escape and grow on, but the tree may already be shaded out by its companions

10 A typical browse line. When investigating any report of damage, care should be taken to establish clearly the species responsible. Sheep, not deer, in this instance

11 Red deer peeling damage to spruce in Glen Branter. Even if the tree survives, the first two meters or more, the most valuable part of the stem, will have been ruined. Damage such as this is frequently caused when red deer break into a plantation and find themselves unable to escape, or where public disturbance inhibits their typical feeding movements

12 Tree shelters recently developed by the Forestry Commission are ideal for use in this type of planting where wide spacing of hardwoods is being used to re-establish a small copse. The shelters not only give protection from deer and rabbits but enhance the trees' growth rates

13 Electric deer fencing. Setting up a fence, in this instance to protect a strip of game cover. A Gallagher high-intensity energiser is used in conjunction with metallic ribbon fencing which is visible day and night

14 Rides in woodland. Where rides have to be made, as for this new power line, the chance should be taken to create open areas with a low growth of scrub on which the deer can feed. Stalking is thus made more productive and these wide rides can also be used to enhance the game shooting

15 Narrow rides soon become overgrown. They never dry out and become mud wallows in the winter. Widening would help to produce an efficient road network in the wood, essential for forestry and for game shooting. The ride sides would become feeding areas for deer

16 A well-constructed wooden high seat. Deer can often be observed at leisure from a high seat as they tend not to look up. Seats also provide a safe, steady shooting position, with the bullet directed into the ground. Nails should not, however, be used to fix the seat to a promising oak tree!

unwanted point of contact must be removed carefully with a rasp. The small areas of contact at the recoil stop and tang should also show a full-width firm contact and, again, careful levelling and shimming with paper may be needed. These are not unnecessary details, but are fundamental to building up the confidence in his rifle which the stalker needs.

(*c*)   Every time the action is taken out of the woodwork, or a screw has been tightened, re-zeroing is necessary. As loose screws are fatal to accuracy, they should all be checked automatically before any zeroing session. In particular the tang and recoil stop screws must be absolutely tight, also the scope mounting blocks, the scope mount clamp screws, and the small screws which clamp the mount rings to the scope tube. A set of Allen keys as well as several carefully-ground turnscrews may be needed. One can now get a set of removable head screwdrivers (4-Shot Ltd, 119 Station Road, Beaconsfield, Bucks.) which is very compact and handy.

Sighting-in
Muntjac and roe deer are very small targets, demanding a high standard of marksmanship if they are to be killed humanely, and with the minimum amount of venison destroyed by the bullet. Even a red stag can have a lot of 'air' round it. Modern scope sights give the stalker invaluable help to aim precisely in order to make full use of the rifle's potential accuracy. None of this is the slightest good if the scope is not adjusted or zeroed so that every shot lands on or very near the aiming mark. A fairly low standard for five shots to lie within is a 10cm (4in) circle at 100m. Lacking confidence in his weapon, or knowing that it is not shooting 'on the nose', any stalker will tend to play safe and aim at the middle of a deer rather than the vital spot. This results in deer being wounded and lost, or at best with large parts of the venison spoiled.

As shown in the table on pp. 98–99 the bullet from a scope-sighted rifle crosses the line of sight twice: Once at about 25m and again at the distance selected. Rough zeroing should be done at the shorter distance where gross errors can be corrected without the likelihood of the bullet missing the target completely. If one careful shot is taken at this range, and the rifle is then clamped with the graticule on the original aiming mark, the adjusting knobs can be turned to *bring the graticule to the shot hole*. This method is easiest

| Calibre | Bullet | | Velocity | | Short Range Bullet does not ris line of sight from | | |
	Weight in grams	Style	Muzzle vel.	Muzzle energy	50 yds	100 yds	150 yds
222 Rem.	50	Hollow Point Power-Lokt	3140	1094	0.5	0.9	(+)
	50	Pointed Soft Point	3140	1094	0.5	0.9	(+)
22–250 Rem.	55	Hollow Point Power-Lokt	3730	1699	0.2	0.5	(+)
		Pointed Soft Point	3730	1699	0.2	0.5	(+)
243 Win.	80	Pointed Soft Point	3420	2077	0.3	0.6	(+)
	100	Pointed Soft Point Core-Lokt	2960	1945	0.5	0.9	(+)
270 Win.	100	Pointed Soft Point	3480	2689	0.3	0.6	(+)
	130	Bronze point	3110	2791	0.4	0.8	(+)
	130	Pointed Soft Point Core-Lokt	3110	2791	0.4	0.7	(+)
	150	Soft Point Core Lokt	2900	2801	0.6	1.0	(+)
7mm Mauser	175	Soft Point	2470	2370	0.4	(+)	−2.
30–06 Springfield	125	Pointed Soft Point	3140	2736	0.4	0.8	(+)
	150	Pointed Soft Point Core-Lokt	2910	2820	0.6	0.9	(+)
	180	Bronze Point	2700	2913	0.2	(+)	−1.
	180	Soft Point Core-Lokt	2700	2913	0.2	(+)	−1.
	220	Soft Point Core-Lokt	2410	2837	0.4	(+)	−2.
308 Win.	150	Pointed Soft Point Core-Lokt	2820	2648	0.2	(+)	−1.
	180	Pointed Soft Point Core-Lokt	2620	2743	0.2	(+)	−1.

Ballistics vary slightly according to the manufacturer.

Trajectory (+) indicates yardage at which rifle is sighted-in										
more than one inch above muzzle to sighting-in range			Long Range Bullet does not rise more than three inches above line of sight from muzzle to sighting-in range							Barrel
200 yds	250 yds	300 yds	100 yds	150 yds	200 yds	250 yds	300 yds	400 yds	500 yds	
−2.4	−6.6	−13.1	2.1	1.8	(+)	−3.6	−9.5	−30.2	−68.1	24in
−2.5	−6.9	−13.7	2.2	1.9	(+)	−3.8	−10.0	−32.3	−73.8	
−1.4	−4.0	−7.7	2.1	2.4	1.7	(+)	−3.0	−13.6	−32.4	24in
−1.5	−4.3	−8.4	2.2	2.6	1.9	(+)	−3.3	−15.4	−37.7	
−1.7	−4.6	−9.0	2.5	2.8	2.0	(+)	−3.4	−15.4	−36.2	24in
−2.2	−5.8	−11.0	1.9	1.6	(+)	−3.1	−7.8	−22.6	−46.3	
−1.6	−4.5	−8.7	2.4	2.7	1.9	(+)	−3.3	−15.0	−35.2	24in
−2.0	−5.3	−10.0	1.7	1.5	(+)	−2.8	−7.1	−20.8	−42.7	
−1.9	−5.1	−9.7	1.7	1.4	(+)	−2.7	−6.8	−19.9	−40.5	
−2.5	−6.8	−13.1	2.2	1.9	(+)	−3.6	−9.3	−28.1	−59.7	
−6.6	−13.4	−23.0	1.5	(+)	−3.6	−9.7	−18.6	−46.8	−92.8	24in
−2.1	−5.6	−10.7	1.8	1.5	(+)	−3.0	−7.7	−23.0	−48.5	
−2.3	−6.3	−12.0	2.1	1.8	(+)	−3.3	−8.5	−25.0	−51.8	
−4.7	−9.6	−16.2	2.4	2.0	(+)	−3.6	−9.1	−26.2	−53.0	
−5.5	−11.2	−19.5	2.7	2.3	(+)	−4.4	−11.3	−34.4	−73.7	
−6.8	−13.8	−23.6	1.5	(+)	−3.7	−9.9	−19.0	−47.4	−93.1	
−4.5	−9.3	−15.9	2.3	1.9	(+)	−3.6	−9.1	−26.9	−55.7	24in
−5.2	−10.4	−17.7	2.6	2.1	(+)	−4.0	−9.9	−28.9	−58.8	

using a Black & Decker 'Workmate' portable vice. Much the same can be done with sandbags on a bench rest or other firm support, but an assistant is needed to move the knobs. The rifle should not of course be fired while clamped. One more shot at short range will confirm that the bullet is on the aiming mark, and a move to longer range can then be made with confidence.

Reference to the ballistic table will show at what range various popular calibres can be zeroed without the bullet being higher than 2.5cm (1in) or 7.6cm (3in) above the line between the muzzle and the given range. Most shots in woodland stalking are at short range and, unless red deer are the target and longer shots expected, the first column will give more satisfactory results. When a quick chance at 50m is offered at a roebuck, it is easy to forget that the bullet is nearly a hand's width high at that range, so that you shoot over his shoulder. Long, deliberate shots, in contrast, give one the time to think about aiming a little high if necessary.

One point often forgotten is that two makes of ammunition cannot be expected to shoot to the same place, although their specifications may be similar. A change of bullet weight will also make a re-check on the range essential. The stalker should make a point of checking his rifle regularly, particularly after a doubtful shot. Oil in the barrel, the chamber or even on the bolt face tends to make the first shot wild. Excessive oil gives very high breech pressures, and may even cause a burst. Since the development of non-corrosive cartridges, few regular stalkers clean their rifles meticulously every day, but maintenance is necessary after a damp day, and to prevent a gradual build-up of residues in the rifling which will destroy accuracy in the long run. After a thorough cleaning, especially if a solvent such as Hoppes No. 9 is used, accuracy will almost certainly be found to have improved, but again, the first shot cannot be relied on. This is everyday stuff to the target shooter, but can make problems for the stalker, whose range facilities may be sketchy or non-existent. For anyone who has perhaps only a week's stalking in the year, finding a safe range and building up his confidence and familiarity with his weapon may well make the difference between success and miserable failure. The ammunition used is an investment which will pay dividends in venison.

Accessories

A non-slip, non-rattle sling must be fitted to the rifle, because it is carried ready for use on the stalker's shoulder. Caps for the scope lenses are essential, preferably taped to the barrel of the scope to avoid getting lost. A leather muzzle cap is good in mud or snow, but sooner or later it gets shot away when something appears suddenly. A piece of sticky tape may be less beautiful, but does the job just as well. For transport, a canvas case large enough to take the rifle with scope attached is useful, protecting the weapon to some extent, and hiding it from prying eyes.

Ammunition can be carried in an old leather tobacco pouch to stop rattles, or in a specially made pouch. A little ingenuity can make up for a tight budget when it comes to the minor items of stalking equipment; knives in particular have become something of a cult, and a serviceable knife made of good steel and with a locking blade can be found at a reasonable price. Sheath knives tend to upset the public and the police, so pocket knives are a safer bet.

Binoculars

Nothing can be achieved without a reliable pair of binoculars, which should be as familiar to the woodland stalker as his rosary is to a priest. Fortunately the capital outlay need not be ruinous. High magnification is a positive disadvantage (7 × or 8 × is more than enough) but large object lenses are needed to give maximum light gathering power at night, with extreme clarity. Although rather bulky, 7 × 50 is regarded as ideal, especially models with universal focus from 10m (30ft) to infinity, as they are very quick to use. Smaller, more compact roof prism glasses with comparable clarity and illumination can be found, but they are extremely expensive and the modestly priced imitations do not in any way measure up to them.

Binocular straps are thin, and the pressure of a heavy pair round the neck hour after hour can be painful. Padding or widening the centre section will help. A piece of leather about 15 × 25cm (6 × 9in) attached to the strap and hanging over the eyepieces will protect them from rain more effectively than the rubber caps normally supplied.

Binoculars are needed to spot deer, to study them to the extent of finding out what they are *thinking* besides what they are doing. Age, sex, condition, and antlers in the case of a buck, must all be observed minutely. Telescopic sights are not suitable and should never be used for this purpose. The most important rule to remember is that a loaded rifle should never be waved about or aimed at unidentified objects.

Telescopes are not often used by woodland stalkers. There are places where spying with the long glass is possible, as one does on the open hill. Sometimes the details of a buck's antlers can be made out, saving a long and fruitless walk if he is not shootable. This applies as much to the wide spaces of chalk downland as to the fringe of the moor.

Clothing and Footwear

Silence is a pre-requisite of woodland stalking, so every item of clothing must have a soft finish, even if waterproofing has to be sacrificed to some extent. The rasp of a bramble or spruce branch against a waxed cotton or nylon jacket is fatal. Old tweeds are good, particularly the loudest patterns, but the 'Kammo' material made by Trueman, Nielsen Ltd, (Bell House, Leamoor Common, Shropshire SY7 8DN) is even better. One can take many more liberties within sight of a deer wearing camouflaged clothes. Plus-two breeches are smart, but midges can penetrate the thickest stockings, and in tick country the wool collects quantities of these detestable creatures. On both counts trousers are better.

When the going is dry, rubber soled shoes are the quietest footwear. One can feel a twig underfoot before it cracks. In long wet grass or boggy ground light-weight rubber boots will be necessary. Traditional, heavy gumboots are too noisy.

The un-selfconscious can wear a loden cloak over everything. Despite the comic-opera flavour, they are excellent garments. They break the human shape, and keep rifle and all dry. Otherwise some sort of waterproof can go in the rucksack for long damp sessions in a high seat. A showerproof tweed hat or cap with a good brim to shade the face completes a practical wardrobe.

A Handy Reminder List

For early morning excursions somnolent stalkers find it prudent to put everything out the night before. Having a typed reminder list in some prominent place may also help to prevent some vital thing being left behind. Everyone will have their own variations on the list which follows:

Rifle, sling, bolt, sight	Rubber gloves
Binoculars	Toilet paper (can also be used to
Compass and map (if in strange	dry/clean binoculars, scope, spectacles)
ground)	Inflatable cushion for high seat
String	Gloves/mittens
Money	Polythene bags
Correct ammunition in pouch	Stalking stick
Knife	Veil
Hat	Paper, pencil
Anti-midge cream	Handkerchief
Calls	Loden cloak
Camera	Rubber boots
Rucksack	Cigarette lighter (for testing direction
Rope	of the wind)

High Seats

High seats are basically platforms from which the stalker can observe and shoot deer more safely and efficiently than from ground level. They have almost become the woodland stalker's trade mark.[30]

Once perched comfortably at a height of 3m (10ft) above the ground in a well-designed and well-sited seat, the stalker is certainly at an advantage over the deer. He can observe them at leisure, and as animals rarely look up, a limited amount of movement is possible. If a shootable animal emerges, a very steady shot can be taken, and because of the angle, the bullet is more likely to bury itself safely in the soil. The semi-aerial view makes it possible to see deer in relatively high plantations that would otherwise be invisible. The design, siting and approach to the seat are all critical to making a relatively expensive structure earn its keep.

Siting

The first and most important point to be decided is whether a seat is necessary to deal effectively with a particular site, or whether the job can be done as well from ground level.

One must be able to approach and climb into the seat unheard and preferably unseen by deer which may be in nearby cover or already out feeding. A ride intersection is good because different routes can be chosen to approach the seat according to the wind. If it is off a ride, then a narrow path, regularly cleared of twigs, must be made.

Place the seat wherever possible so that it neither faces the morning nor the evening sun, and always plan the arcs of fire with safety in mind. Shooting straight down a ride towards an intersection, or across a clearing towards a footpath, the stalker may find without warning that he can see his buck and a party of birdwatchers in his telescopic sight at one time.

Wherever possible there should be a background of trees so that the seat and its occupant are not silhouetted against the sky. A few bushes left untrimmed at the base also help to mask the final approach and ascent. To make the best use of a small number of portable seats, prepare several sites in different parts of the forest, so that a seat can be moved easily from one to the other as need arises without having to disturb the local deer by cutting branches or clearing scrub.

Types of high seat

Seats are either self-standing or designed to be supported by a tree (lean-to). Some are heavy permanent structures, others are portable, or at least movable. The type of woodland dictates to some extent what seats are likely to be the most useful. Clearly lean-to seats are not suitable for areas of young plantations. In fact a very substantial tree is needed before they can be relied

A timber lean-to seat easily made from local materials. The poles should have the bark removed and the rungs should be notched into the uprights

on not to sway slightly in a wind. Shooting from a seat which is swaying, no matter how slightly, reduces marksmanship to something approaching shooting pin-pong balls on a jet of water.

A permanent seat needs to be erected where its usefulness is certain to last: overlooking an established clearing for example, at a major ride intersection, or in an already well-thinned plantation. Semi-permanent types are best suited to covering newly-planted and vulnerable plantations. One move during the life of the seat can be planned after four or five years when the trees grow tall enough to hide a deer. For versatility, and for experiment to see whether a fixed seat would be justified, the portable seat is unrivalled. Some really do pack into a rucksack and are ideal for the weekend stalker. Others take half an hour of spanner work to erect, and often a great deal more to take down, especially if they have been left up some time. A liberal hand with the grease on any sliding or close-fitting parts is the only hope with steel seats.

Design
A general purpose high seat needs to perch the stalker about 3m (10ft) above ground level. It must be stout enough to comply with industrial safety regulations, sufficiently comfortable for a stay of several hours, and fitted with some form of rail on which the shooter can rest his hand to obtain a

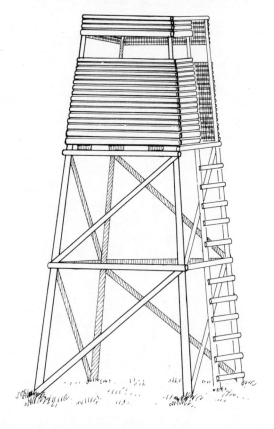

'Thetford high seat (Forestry Commission)

An excellent design of double-sided seat

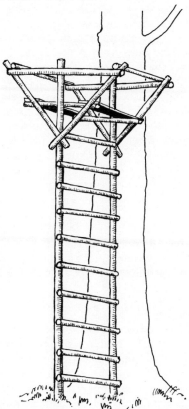

steady shot. The type consisting of a wooden box on four legs should have shooting slits so that there is no movement over the top of the box. Other types can be draped with foliage or camouflage netting to conceal the stalker. This seems to be more important with fallow than with other species. A roof is luxury indeed, but may make the seat more used, and thus more profitable. The material used for roofing is important. Something resonant like corrugated iron prevents the occupier from hearing anything during a shower. The floors of box seats tend to get slimy with bird droppings. A square of wire netting tacked down is a good safety measure.

The public and poachers have an affinity with high seats, and employers should be mindful of their obligations even to trespassers. Portable seats may be the only answer, though in some woods there are sufficient ancient trees in which to construct platforms. The ladder can be taken away. Unfortunately the right tree is very rarely in the right place, and high seat placing rarely allows a compromise. A towable, mobile high seat on a trailer chassis has recently been developed which has great potential in well-roaded forests.

Very large observation hides, holding a dozen or so people, are in use in some forests to accommodate parties of naturalists. Recreational use can also be made of ordinary seats out of the stalking season by photographers and others.

One important decision is whether to go in for single- or two-seaters. If there is any question of letting stalking in the future, two-man seats are needed to accommodate stalker and visitor.

Factory-made high seats are made to fit and bear the average man. Home-made models, in contrast, are often well-adapted to the stalker's own physique. If the rungs of the ladder are rather far apart, he is lithe and active enough to have no difficulty, and may be surprised when an elderly visitor runs into trouble. Sitting on a plank seat which is just the right height for a tall man is agony to one of lesser stature, and the shooting position can also be awkward, and lead to loss of accuracy. A considerate professional will bear these points in mind when constructing his seats.

Getting into a seat smoothly and in silence is made easier if the ladder rungs are close together, easier still if the ladder itself is inclined rather than vertical. Metal structures are inevitably noisy. A length of garden hosepipe, split and fitted over the shooting rail is some help. Unload the rifle when climbing into a seat.

Lack of confidence in the safety of the seat itself or its fastenings is demoralising; four-legged models should be dug in, and in exposed places secured with guy wires at each corner. If a lean-to seat sways in the wind, the supporting tree can sometimes be topped (with the forester's approval!) which stops the trouble.

Materials and maintenance

Some seats are manufactured from light alloy or light-weight steel tube. The latter need regular inspection for rust, missing bolts or stiff hinges. Internal rust can lead to unexpected failure, and frost has been known to split the tubes. A coat of preservative paint should be applied and the sliding joints must be regreased. Lean-to seats in long-term sites may have chafed or loose attachments to the supporting tree. These seats are most suitable for short-term use, and benefit from dry storage. The component parts of some makes are not interchangeable and sets should be marked and kept together.

Making a seat from green timber is labour in vain, as its effective life will be measured in months rather than years before rot makes it dangerous. A seat made from timber which has been pressure-creosoted or treated with a chemical preservative on the contrary should last at least 15 years, though it should be checked thoroughly every season. A knife thrust in at ground level will show if the main supports are still sound. Ladder rungs, being thinner material tend to rot, and stalking visitors often heavy and unfit, tread powerfully on them. There are few more alarming sights for a professional stalker than to see his visitor descending involuntarily from above by breaking successive rungs. The stool or plank on which one sits should be tested, and maybe modified with extra comfort in mind. An empty five-gallon drum lowers the tone, and is agony after the first hour. A broad plank is better than a narrow one, or a bench made up of round and knobbly timbers.

'Housekeeping' is the term for work round about a seat which makes it useful or not. Approach paths need to be trimmed and cleared of twigs; bushes which have grown too tall need cutting or topping. Maybe the roof leaks or the salt lick needs renewing. Most important are the branches which need pruning to improve visibility. As the leaves come in spring, branches that were well out of the way in winter suddenly droop down. A long-handled pruning saw will probably be needed, and the work can be done quickly by a two-man team, one in the seat pointing out to the other which branches need to go. Seats that have been condemned should be pulled down and broken up without delay to avoid accidents.

A yearly deadline for inspection and maintenance of seats is essential. In roe areas it should be in March, before the buck season, otherwise in late summer. Responsibility is shared by employer and employee to ensure that high seats conform to current regulations. These lay down, among other things, that rungs must be notched in and wired down, and that guard rails are provided. The Forestry Commission's publication *High Seats for Deer Control* (1979)[30] gives the following references:

Agriculture (Ladders) Regulations 1957 (S.1 1385);

Construction (Working Places) Regulations 1966 (S.1 94);

Health & Safety at Work etc. Act 1974.

Removing the Carcase from the Forest

Happy is the stalker of roe or muntjac! With a rucksack slung on his back he can go out alone and have no second thoughts about getting his game home safely and easily. Even a 22kg (50lb) roebuck makes no unbearable weight over a mile or more, and the larger roe sacks can even accommodate a couple of does. 60 × 50cm (2ft × 1ft 8in) is a good size. Two waterproof liners are needed, so that one can do duty when the other is washed and drying. In an emergency the buck's legs can be tied together with a piece of string, and the carcase slung over one shoulder.

Problems tend to multiply when the larger deer have to be humped out of the wood. The single-handed stalker has either to cut down his chances by shooting only where he can get a vehicle reasonably near, or make arrangements beforehand to get help when needed. A few simple items of equipment can be carried or left in the car which will alleviate some of the backbreaking toil involved, let alone the risk of physical injury, in dragging or lifting a dead deer which may weigh between 50 and 200kg (100 and 400lb). The simplest is a dragging rope, thick enough to give a good grip and not cut into the shoulder. The Swedes use ropes for dragging moose which have a spring clip (carabiner) at one end, and well-made handle at the other which can be pulled with both hands. Two can also be clipped together by means of a ring.

A two-man plastic carrying sack is available which will accommodate about four roe or one or two fallow does. Even one man would find the slick plastic easier to drag than the deer alone. The same idea has been utilised by the Forestry Commission in developing their deer sledge, which is basically a square of robust plastic with roped edges. A red stag can be dragged with one tenth of the effort on this sheet, though it is only suitable for grassy areas without exposed rocks to rip or wear it. The latest design incorporates lengths of old transmission belting (about 150 × 75cm [5ft × 2ft 6in]) which reduces wear on rough ground. There are hopes that these sledges can be pulled by the three-wheel cross-country motor bikes now available. To make this feasible, forest design will have to take account for the need for reasonably smooth access.

Obviously where many deer have to be shot each year some form of mechanical transport is justified. A tractor and link box saves lifting, and can often be spared from other work when needed for this purpose. Landrovers and similar vehicles can be fitted with a capstan, or a small electric winch in the rear compartment.

Small cross-country machines used extensively on the open hill to recover deer are at a disadvantage in the forest where the land will probably have been ploughed for planting, or at least drained. Once the carcase has been brought to a ride, it can probably be collected with a faster and more conventional vehicle. A Danish deerkeeper devised a very effective machine for use in flat country, which resembled a miniature timber arch, with two wheels and a long drawbar. It was towed behind a car to the nearest road point, then under power provided by a motor cycle engine and gear box, it could be steered at walking pace through the trees. The stag's head was attached to the arch, and the carcase towed out easily in low gear. Over the water in Sweden the elk stalker has a great problem. One idea they have developed is a sort of backless boat made of fibreglass which can be dragged along fairly easily by three or four hunters, even when loaded with 500kg of elk.[31] A scaled-down version might be very handy in this country.

Larders and Cold Stores

Venison is a valuable commodity, and the regulations regarding hygiene are becoming quite rightly more strict. Stalkers are now subject to the provisions of the Food Safety Act and the European Wild Game Meat Directive which impose hygiene standards from the time of shooting onwards. The heart, lungs and liver should be available, labelled to identify the respective carcase. Clean conditions in the larder are required, and full slaughterhouse specifications must be followed for premises where deer are skinned and butchered. The walls and floor of any larder must be washable. Water should be available, and rats, mice, cats and flies rigidly excluded.

Lifting even a roe carcase up to an awkward hook or rail can be dangerous: ruptures, slipped discs and gashed hands are common accidents in poorly designed larders. One of the most widespread errors is to have insufficient headroom over the rail. Roe are often sold head and legs on, and if they are hung by the hocks, at least 40cm (1ft 4in) is needed to allow for the length of leg, and to give a clear lift.

Larger deer make lifting tackle essential, both for the space where they are dressed and in the larder, unless a transfer rail is installed. For occasional use, a multi-purchase block and tackle such as that sold by Armstrongs (Gunmakers) Ltd (360 Carlton Hill, Nottingham) is quite sufficient. Given a stout rail or beam 2m to 2.2m (6ft 6in to 7ft 6in) above ground level even quite a large stag can be lifted and suspended for skinning or storage, provided that the pulley rope is thick enough not to be painful to haul. Some small blocks have so many pulley wheels that the mechanical advantage is lost in friction.

Where deer are regularly handled a permanent hoist is much better. Small geared hand winches can be bought from yacht chandlers and they are ideal for the purpose. The winch is bolted to the larder wall, and the rope led over a high pulley, to hang near the beam.

Meat hooks must be made of stainless steel, strong enough for the largest carcase with considerable margin to allow for the tugging involved in skinning. Tinned iron hooks go rusty, and are potentially dangerous. When working on a carcase it is better suspended with a hook on each leg to avoid swinging. The traditional gambrel is satisfactory for neat storage in the larder.

Better prices are often obtainable from the game dealer if deer can be kept in a cold store, and collected at convenient intervals. Forests handling many deer in the summer and early autumn can invest with confidence in a small prefabricated cold store, interconnected with the larder and sited where power and water are available, where the dealer's van can be driven up easily, and not in such an isolated place to make a break-in likely. The fairly substantial cost will be offset by the turnover of venison at an enhanced price.

Failing a purpose-built cold store, various insulated vehicle bodies can be purchased second hand which will serve the purpose. An ice-cream van or meat container is easily found and transported to the site. Hanging rails should be fitted, if they are not already there, and a small chiller unit fitted in with the compressor and motor outside, but sheltered from the weather. This is better bought separately, as the units commonly found on vehicles are not likely to be suitable, and may in fact be for three-phase 440-volt supply.

The same rules for hygiene, easy lifting and adequate headroom apply in the cold store as for larders. Transfer rails between larder and cold store are ideal, though thought must be given to a removable section for the doorway. When designing the lay-out it is better to have a level run of the rail between the two, even if this means a step up into the larder because the door is not tall enough. Two-inch water piping makes a satisfactory rail, or sliding door gear can be used.

Floors should be sloped to a gulley along one wall which discharges to a large external trap. Some local authorities insist on some form of septic tank for the effluent. A pressure hose is essential for every larder, and washing facilities with a small water heater are required by industrial regulations.

All this may seem unnecessarily complicated, but venison is now a high-priced commodity. One carcase rejected by the dealer represents a large loss, just as a higher price throughout the year justifies a reasonable investment.

Trophies

Preparation

The amateur stalker is free to take an interest in trophies or disregard them in the interests of having a dust-free house, but they are of considerable importance to the professional. Failure to produce clean-boiled and properly bleached skulls at the end of a hard week's stalking will leave the visitor with a poor impression, nor is the stalker likely to be enriched at the same time. Since the days when the antlers and feet of deer were turned into everything from chairs to inkstands, our interest in trophies waned and has only recently been revived as part of the current passion for Victoriana. With the majority of visitors from Europe trophies are a consuming passion which the stalker underestimates at his peril.

From the moment a male deer is shot, no matter how insignificant its antlers may appear to a detached and knowledgeable eye, time and consideration must be given to the guest, who will want to bathe in the triumph of the moment. This is what he has come a long way to do, and the moment must not be spoiled by a brisk gralloch and pointed remarks about breakfast. Some countries, notably Germany and Austria, incline to ceremonial, and it does no harm to learn the few words and actions which will bring a great deal of additional pleasure to the visitor. If they go too far in respect for a dead beast, maybe we do not go far enough.

If an exceptional trophy is shot, the owner may want to have it mounted. If he does, one needs to find this out at a very early stage because the skin must be cut differently. The underside of the neck is left intact, and a cut made from between the shoulders to between the ears. From this line the skin is peeled off, leaving nearly half the pelt attached to the neck cape. Taxidermists never have enough skin. Once the head and cape have been detached, they should be rushed to the taxidermist, or very quickly frozen. Fortunately, all is not lost if the skin is wrongly cut, or the hair is not perfect. Another buck can be shot later on, selected for being in perfect pelage, rather than for its antlers.

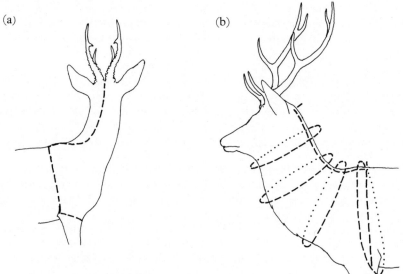

(a)   (b)

Mike Windham-Wright, formerly the head of Zimmermans in Nairobi, and now working from his home in Argyllshire, gives this advice:

With a very sharp knife, so as to obtain a good clean cut, make the first incision between the shoulder blades. Cut straight up the middle of the back of the neck to where it joins the head. Be very careful not to cut the hair, so that the stitching can be concealed when it is mounted. Then cut from the shoulder right round the sides of the body behind the front leg. Then round the front leg as shown in diagram (a). It is important to have plenty of skin, as the taxidermist has to have enough to fold round the back of the form. Skin out the neck up to the head, taking care not to make any holes.

At this stage it is very useful for the taxidermist if you take measurements of the neck as shown in diagram (b). It is also helpful to have photographs of the animal just after it has been killed. After measuring, sever the head from the top of the neck and roll up the neck skin. Be very careful not to soil the flesh with mud or dirt while skinning as game dealers will object.[32]

Full mounting apart, the normal preparation of trophies consisting of the antlers and skull is very much the stalker's province. He must remember to leave time for photography; there is little more embarrassing than for the happy visitor to return to the stalker's house after a celebratory breakfast, camera in hand, only to find his buck already dismembered, and the trophy boiling in a rather unsavoury pot.

Speed can be important if the guest is departing, but otherwise 24 hours immersed in a bucket of cold water does make a good start to preparing the head. The job cannot be put off longer than that, for a run of luck can pile up the work. If he has been putting things off from day to day the stalker may find himself with a dozen very smelly heads to prepare late on Friday night.

Most skulls are shortened by cutting on a line through the eye sockets, but tastes vary and the visitor must be asked what he likes, if he cannot be persuaded to do the job himself! The standard cut for all species is from the top of the articulation with the first vertebra through the eye socket to emerge at the nose. A 'long nose' cut removes the lower part of the brain pan and the upper teeth, but leaves the front part of the palate and the two oval bones forming the nose. The lower jaw is always boiled out and bleached, and attached to the trophy.

A cutting jig can be bought which simplifies the job, but care is needed to adjust it. It is prudent to experiment with a cull buck's head before risking a valued trophy. Otherwise the best way is to lay the skinned head on its side on a firm bench, holding the antlers in one hand, so that the line can be chosen. When cutting has gone far enough to hold the saw, sight along the blade to see where it is due to emerge. If it is going crooked, do not finish this cut, but start again from the opposite side. Irregularities can be levelled off after boiling with a power grindstone. The best saw for the purpose is a broad-bladed woodsaw, rather than a tenon or meat saw.

Most roe go to the game dealer with head and legs on, and removing the head represents a substantial loss. In Poland they remove the antlers and the top of the skull without detaching the head, then by a little crude stitchery replace the flaps of skin and the ears to a semblance of nature. The game dealer might consider himself hard done by if he were not consulted first, at least if full price is expected.

Another method of detaching the antlers is to hang the entire buck from a stout nail driven into a post. This nail is lodged under the point of the buck's jaw, thus holding the head steady for sawing. A knife-cut through the fur should always be made to indicate the right line for the saw-cut and to avoid jamming the teeth.

Once roughly skinned and cut, the skull is immersed in boiling water, but not the antlers. Clamps can be bought which make this easier. About 40g per litre (6oz per gallon) of washing soda in the water shortens the cooking time and starts the process of degreasing. When the shreds of flesh have a jelly-like appearance, the skull can be rapidly cleaned, using an old knife as a scraper and a pair of strong bent-nose pliers. All the skull contents must be removed, and also the fine network of bones in the nasal cavity. As soon as all is clean, cover the skull with a thin layer of cotton wool or tissue and soak it with domestic Hydrogen peroxide. Mature skulls will benefit by 12 hours soaking. When the wool is removed, the bone should be bleached and practically odour-free.

If several heads are being boiled in the same pot, some means of matching

skull to jawbone must be devised such as a certain number of twists of tying wire. When all is dry, each trophy must be labelled with the date, place and time shot, the name of the shooter and the estimated age. The jawbone is attached, and is important in any discussions on age. The whole jaw, not just the teeth, should be kept. Otherwise much of the evidence will be thrown away.

Boiling heads is a smelly job, which cannot be expected to go on in the kitchen. A boiling ring in the workshop or garage is essential. Aluminium pots should not be used, as the soda will ruin them.

Shields for mounting can be purchased, or simply made to any pattern which appeals to the owner. Oblique slices off a seasoned birch log are very effective. If enough bone has been left, there will be a solid bridge between the eye sockets which will hold a No. 8 woodscrew through the shield. This

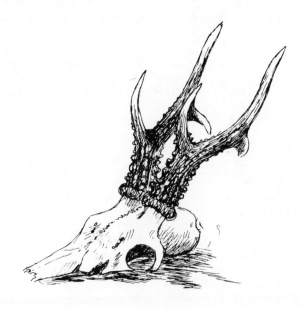

gives a neat, invisible fixing. If the cut was too high for this, drill a hole behind the pedicles rather than in the visible part of the skull. The shield can be hung up by using a slotted brass glass plate.

Deer skins are so pretty that people want to preserve them. Unfortunately the hair is very fragile and no matter how carefully the tanning is done, any wear will make them bald. Anyone determined to try should preferably find an accommodating professional tanner or taxidermist, or failing that, put the skin as soon as possible in 5 per cent formalin (obtainable from chemists) for seven days. In the meanwhile get a supply of a proprietory skin dressing compound, and follow the instructions. It is a fairly laborious process, and success cannot be guaranteed. Buckskin has, of course, long been admired as leather. A friendly tanner is again indicated. One of the problems is that most wild deer have come into contact with barbed wire and so on, which mars the leather. Scottish red deer skins are likely to have been ruined with warble holes.

Legs, which some stalkers like to make into coat hooks, can be tied to the right shape and left in methylated spirit for several months. The shank bone is cut off square, and then an opposed-thread screw (Rawlplug) serves to attach the hook to the wall. A spray with anti-moth from time to time is essential.

Measuring

Having shot a good head, the successful stalker often wants to know how it measures up against local, national, or even world standards. This can be done comparatively easily through the judging rules for International trophy exhibitions developed by the Conseil International de la Chasse (C.I.C.). Formulae for each deer species have been published[33] and

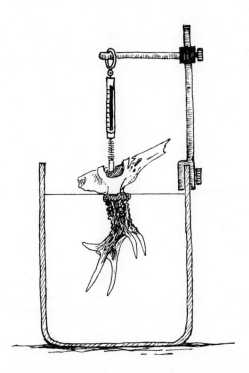

standards for Gold, Silver and Bronze medals are given. To achieve an official score, a trophy has to be exhibited at an International Exhibition, but an unofficial score can be obtained by arranging for a head to be measured by the British Deer Society. They also issue their own medals for qualifying trophies, which are in great demand, especially by visiting sportsmen.

For accurate measurement, the skull must have been shot more than 3 months, to allow for drying out, but an approximation can be made by allowing 10 per cent for eventual loss of weight on a trophy which is boiled out and dry, but still 'green'.

The accepted standards for our deer species are as follows:

	Gold	Silver	Bronze	World* Record	British* Record
Red	210+	190–209.9	170–189.9	261.25	197.67
Fallow	180+	175–179.9	165–174.9	220.31	186.17
Sika	250+	240–249.9	225–239.9	307.3	295.1
Roe	130+	115–129.9	105–114.9	228.68	210.25
Muntjac †	56+	55–55.9	54–54.9	78.7	58.7

* At the Budapest Exhibition of 1971, a special category was created for Scottish red deer as follows:

Bronze: 160–167.9; Silver: 168–179.9; Gold 180+.

† Muntjac as exhibited at the International Hunting Exhibition at Plovdiv 1981.

Section III

Deer Management

11 *Management Aims and Priorities*

If deer are to play a productive part in the forest economy as a potential asset, consideration must be given to the aims of management: what concessions other forms of land use have to make because of the unavoidable presence of deer, and to what extent these concessions or direct expenditure can be balanced by income from them.

Contrary to some current schools of thought, deer and forestry are inseparably intertwined. The very fact that deer are now more numerous than ever in the United Kingdom is due to the enormous expansion of forestry since the Second World War. Afforestation creates new cover.

Felling and replanting give the undergrowth and food without which the deer population would naturally fall. The way the forest is managed affects the resident population of deer just as deer management, or the lack of it, can fundamentally affect the forest. Economical timber production is always likely to be the first priority, but not regardless of the cost-effectiveness of forestry operations, nor of other considerations such as amenity, landscape, or in the smaller woodlands, the sporting potential which can easily rival the claims of straight commercial cellulose production.

The aims of management will normally fall into the following three headings, and in this order of priority:

1   Reduce damage
2   Keep deer population healthy and in
    balance with food and cover available
3   Balance expenditure by harvesting a crop:
(a)   Venison
(b)   Sport
(c)   Recreation (deer watching, photography)

Reduction of Damage

While deer are present, some damage will be done. The intention should be to keep damage to an acceptable level where it can be balanced by the various forms of harvest from the deer. It should be clear by now that this can only be achieved by planning and collaboration at all stages between forester and deer manager.

Healthy Deer

Since deer lack major predators, can we 'let nature take its course', or is deer control essential? The fact is that the only natural controls left are starvation and disease. The most ardent advocate of the balance of nature would presumably shrink from condemning several hundred thousand deer a year to death from starvation, yet deer control is sometimes criticised by the unthinking as unnecessary and cruel. In addition, the damage to farming and forestry would be quite unacceptable long before the deer ate themselves into extinction. Even in the Yellowstone National Park, where by statute no animal could be killed, a severe programme of culling had, in the end, to be authorised because the elk had become so numerous that all the browse was eaten out.

Accepting that the deer must be kept within the capacity of the forest to support them without undue damage, three alternatives are offered:

1   To feed the deer by hand, and thus reduce
damage while maintaining an artificially high
population

2   To reduce the deer population to such a low
level that interference with normal forest
operations is minimal

3   To increase the natural food available, and at the
same time reduce the population to the point where
naturally growing food is sufficient to avoid
serious forest damage.

Hand feeding

Hand feeding is accepted in many continental countries, especially those where winters are severe and shooting rents high. While it does produce heavy trophies, forest damage can by no means be ruled out, and may well be increased as was mentioned in Chapter 3.

It is no part of the intention of this book to advocate the maintenance of an unnaturally high population at the expense of the forest enterprise, nor are the present returns from deer likely to justify it. If hand feeding is embarked upon, it will be to cater for an unusual situation, and must be planned as an integral part of intensive deer management. Sporadic feeding in time of scarcity is pointless. By the time the digestive system of the deer has become adapted to a novel type of feed, the animal will be dead of starvation, though with a full belly, or with the vagaries of our climate the weather will have changed and natural food will once more be available.

Red deer and fallow do take readily to hand feeding, and significant improvement in body weight, productivity and trophy size can be expected. When venison and trophy prices have appreciated from their present levels, hand feeding may be financially justified, even allowing for the risk of increased forest damage. In deer parks, and where deer are intensively farmed other considerations apply.

Extensive reduction of the deer population

Reducing the deer population to an insignificant level is the ambition of many foresters who feel that their profession is compromised by the presence of deer. Unless the deer are integrated into the total concept of forestry, and their harvest included with that of timber, there is conflict indeed; not only because of the damage done by deer, but because of the cost of deer control operations in the absence of any compensating revenue, or of the flexible understanding in forest design and planning which was covered in Section I.

There will be a tendency to regard the deer as 'vermin' to be eliminated by all means and at all times. Without sympathetic forest design the 'deer problem' will build up and with the increase of damage more effort will be put into harrying them, at first every day in the season, then as they become even more secretive, in the close season and at night. Men asked to do this become tired, dispirited and sickened by the slaughter of females in milk, fawns and promising males.

Shooting deer at night has been widely advocated as a certain technique for reducing deer numbers quickly and economically. At first it was promoted as a remote possibility, only to be used in rare cases of real emergency against red deer, then more openly as a legitimate option for the hard-pressed forester. In fact the effectiveness of night shooting has never been tested, even on red deer, as a means of *radically reducing* the population of a forest block. Until proved otherwise, informed opinion takes the view that the deer will quickly become as shy at night as during the day, and night shooting will not be cost-effective. The other real problems of safety, risk of wounding, shooting two at once, etc., are discussed elsewhere.

Income from Deer

Integrating the return from timber and deer is the only route to logical compromise between the two, each bearing its part in the forest's productivity. Fencing them out is no long-term solution, for the fence will be breached or decay sooner or later, and a resident population will become established.

Concessions to deer by the forester may be justified on financial terms apart from the need to control damage. Arthur Witchell, a qualified land agent gave an interesting factual sample in a survey of 69 hectares (170 acres) of woodland in Wiltshire.[34]

The aims of the deer management are:
(*1*)   to minimise fraying damage to the planted conifers, and
(*2*)   produce an income for the owner.

(*1*)   is achieved by liaising with the forester and leaving plenty of natural scrub for territory marking by the bucks, and by carefully selecting the bucks to cull.
(*2*)   is achieved in the annual sum of venison sales, less expenses, of over £100. This income if invested at 5 per cent will compound to £45,000 by year 65. This return is equivalent to seven acres of 65-year-old Yield Class 20 Norway Spruce at today's prices. So a reasonable income from deer can always justify some part of a woodland being managed with the deer in mind.

Increasing the natural food, especially in places where the deer can be observed, as suggested in Section II, increases the potential return, improves the efficiency of deer control operations and at the same time reduces the liability of the main crop to damage.

If one regards deer as a renewable resource, as indeed they are, then proper conservation involves an annual harvest, to balance the cost of damage or control. Venison, as mentioned above, is a significant element. By-products such as antlers, skins, deer hair, sinews, tails and pizzles are all marketable. The sport of shooting also has a ready market, mostly from continental sportsmen, which is perfectly legitimate provided that the visitor is supervised, and that he is not permitted to shoot animals outside the shooting plan, over-exploiting middle-aged males at the expense of proper management. If the stalking of these quality males is let separately from the other and more essential part of the management plan – juvenile males and females – then not only should the price reflect this, but every effort should be made to attract capable local stalkers to complete the cull. The benefit of this to the owner is measured in venison sales and reduced forest damage, not high fees.

In certain places deer may be caught up by baiting them into enclosures from which a reasonable proportion can be sold off for re-stocking deer parks and farms. This method may also have to be considered in built-up areas, or where public pressure is very high, either to protect the deer, as with the Epping fallow deer, or as a control measure where shooting might be dangerous.

Venison sales

Meat production from wild deer cannot of course be regulated as it can be on a farm. A near-natural sex ratio has to be maintained to keep the social stability of the herd, and to provide for herd replacements, allowing for natural mortality. A seriously unbalanced sex ratio or age-class structure can lead to increased damage. This does mean that some males will have to be retained after their period of maximum weight gain (18 months from birth) to be culled out as adults. These have a sporting or trophy value which may be realised by including a sporting element in the management policy. Within these limits, red fallow and sika deer can be successfully managed with ratios of one male to two or three females (as shown in the Table) which of course will increase the productivity of the herd *provided there is enough food and provided the surplus is actually harvested.* Otherwise the ratio should be as near as possible to 1:1 to reduce the overall productivity and in the hope of bigger unit weights. In deer parks (semi-intensive management) a ratio of 1:6 or 1:7 can be maintained if venison production is the sole objective.

Production and Sex Ratio

Red Deer – Shooting Plan Related to Various Sex Ratios

	1:1	1:2	1:3
Stags	534	356	267
Hinds	534	712	801
Total	1068	1068	1068
Calves	224	299	336
Mortality	64	68	70
Crop	160	231	266
As % of Pop.	12.5	17	19

De Nahlik[35]

Venison prices over the last two decades have risen under the influence of demand from Europe. They have also fluctuated, to the despair of producer and dealer alike. A domestic market is slowly developing which will help to stabilise prices. The producer has the option of selling to a game dealer, or of taking a licence and marketing his venison locally. In the latter case he will have to consider the labour of skinning and selling; the small proportion of a carcase which can readily be sold as joints, and the possible loss of saleable meat through bullet damage. Not least the requirements of various hygiene regulations which come into force where venison is cut up and sold.

The building and plumbing work involved in bringing a larder up to the required standard is only likely to be justified by a major turnover. Even overnight storage for unskinned beasts has to conform to a reasonable standard of cleanliness, sealed against flies, rats, mice and cats. Selling occasional single carcases to a game dealer will not attract the best prices, especially if he has to collect them from a distance. Even so, a reasonable spirit of healthy competition between two dealers should keep them in order. A reputation for well-shot and properly prepared carcases will go a long way. No dealer can be expected to collect dirty, contaminated or spoiled venison and still pay highly for it.

Where the number of deer shot is significant the merits of cold storage should be examined. Because the dealer need only collect every week, or at his convenience following a call, he will be prepared to offer a lead over the ordinary rate, or even put in his own semi-portable equipment. Cold stores are preferred to deep freezers because the deer do not have to be thawed out.

If some form of cold store is installed, it can sometimes be shared with neighbours to spread the cost. Commercial cold stores exist in many large towns in which space can be rented. Deer can be delivered there for collection by the dealer.

Consultation with the dealer is necessary at the beginning of each season, and he may also advise on the preparation and sale of some by-products. Sales by tender or contract have so far proved less than satisfactory because of the volatility of the market. It is better to make sure of the current price by an enquiring phone call to a competitor from time to time.

Live sales

The market for live deer, having reached a peak in the 1980s crashed when BSE disease in cattle ended the export trade. When prices pick up again, live capture for sale may be worth consideration. To make the exercise worthwhile a narrow enclosure must be made into which the deer can be lured and held. Once saleable deer have been enclosed, they can be darted with comparative ease, and the price offered improves accordingly. The problem is that the deer caught and sold are likely to be prime breeding stock, and so live sales from a park herd should be limited to the number of prime females which can be spared each year, or the sale should be restricted to alternate years. Culling of old and poor specimens must still continue.

12 *Letting Stalking*

Woodland deer stalking represents the last unexploited asset on many estates. If stalking is developed as part of the management plan it will mean that there is an expert deer controller to limit forest damage, that a full-time gamekeeper will not have to be sacked for lack of funds, and that a private shoot can still be enjoyed without being forced to syndicate it or to let days.

The head keeper on one large estate in the south was in the habit of shooting about six roe for the house each year. When times were hard, and the possibility of having to sack a beat keeper loomed up, advice was taken on the roe stalking and a suitable tenant was found. Within three years sufficient had been raised from rent and sales of venison to save his job. Not all letting possibilities will be on this scale, but proper management and marketing of deer on the shoot or estate can produce an unexpected and often valuable return.

The priorities of deer management should not be set aside in the heedless pursuit of revenue. Damage limitation still heads the list, and the male deer should not be over-exploited for short-term gain. The time to investigate letting in any form is when the deer population is under reasonable control, and the man responsible for culling is fully trained, knows his ground and is not already over-stressed by the need to achieve a very large target.

Having reached this stage the questions which any woodland manager should investigate before deciding to let stalking are as follows:

1   Is letting possible?
Is damage under control?
Is stalker fully trained?
Are stalking rights unencumbered?
Is there conflict with other land use?

2   What type of let?
Block let or short-term?

3   Short term – How many visitors?
Duration of stalking lets?
Number of deer available for letting?
When can visitors be accommodated?
How do you work out the rent and conditions?

4   Who will cope with the paper-work?

The Possibility of Letting

Every estate and forest block has its own individual set of circumstances and personalities to which deer management options have to be adapted. Where, for example, there is little liability to damage and no alternative work which an employed deer keeper might usefully do in his spare time, a low input and low return may be suitable, with the tenant committed to doing all the work himself, or accepting the liability to pay a deer stalker himself. This is usually the case where the area or the number of deer to be shot each year is small, or where two or more estates are leased by one shooting tenant to make a shoot which is large enough to support a full-time deer keeper.

Small woods lend themselves admirably to the attentions of the amateur enthusiast, many of whom are extremely skilled and responsible, and have sufficient time to cope adequately with bucks and does. Many such stalking propositions are quite unlettable because of public disturbance, or the need for extreme care when shooting. In these the stalker is performing a service for the landowner. Elsewhere, a modest return can be expected either in the form of rent or venison or both.

Care must always be taken, both by lessor and intending lessee, that the right to shoot deer is actually in the lessor's hands, and that it is unencumbered. A farm tenant suffering from the attentions of deer may be glad to give any stalker permission to go and shoot them, forgetting that his landlord may have an equal or even an exclusive right. Almost all land leased to the Forestry Commission gives them, as tenants, a concurrent right to kill deer, though the conditions vary and should be investigated. In particular, some old leases give the right to kill deer, but not to carry them away. Obviously this creates an anomalous situation but negotiation between parties can often result in a satisfactory outcome. Nothing could be more embarrassing than for two stalkers to go for the same buck, both believing themselves in the right. If they start from opposite sides of the field, it is also dangerous. No letting is possible without agreement between all the parties concerned.

Letting also implies reasonably free access to the ground, even if the hours are laid down in the agreement. If other activities, camping sites, pony trekking, small game shooting or anything of the sort take priority at weekends or certain seasons, then these constraints must be openly declared even if the value of the stalking is reduced. In many places a system of zoning will have to be thought out. One estate where the roe stalking has been let successfully for several years is divided into three categories in the stalking agreement:

1   No access at any time (gardens, park, stud farm paddocks)

2   No access at specified times or seasons (the vicinity of racehorse exercise gallops, copses containing pheasant release pens, and camping sites)

3   Access during normal stalking hours.

These areas were clearly marked on a map forming part of the agreement.

Block Letting

The advantages of having a long-term tenant who becomes familiar with the ground and takes an interest in the management of his deer are obvious. Administrative costs are small compared to short-term letting, and supervision can be reduced as the tenant earns the confidence of the estate. The right man will shoot what is good for the stock, and leave promising males for the future, while the day visitor will want to shoot something in his short stay. The problem is in fact that block tenants may not be willing, or have sufficient time, to shoot enough for the good of the forest, and stringent safeguards need to be built into this agreement.

Suggested Heads of Agreement for a block let are included in the Reference Section, and each clause should be carefully considered in the light of local needs.

Many continentals are accustomed to a set term of years for a stalking let, usually seven or nine years, and are suspicious of anything shorter, or open-ended. In spite of this, a trial year is recommended, and if the tenant proves himself, he can be offered either a three- or five-year licence with regular rent reviews, or an open-ended yearly licence with an option to renew. Rent reviews can even then be specified at given dates.

In England a formal lease attracts rates, while yearly licences do not. Scottish rating law has a different basis, and rates are levied on sporting values. If the lessor is registered, there will be a liability to VAT at current rates on the rent, but not on venison. If the lessor runs a shoot, and therefore has a Game Account, which will almost certainly be in deficit, he will be well advised to retain the venison rather than take a higher rent.

In phrasing the letting agreement, the main object should be to retain as much control as possible, while still achieving the maximum rent. Sub-letting by the tenant is one particularly difficult field. One can find that so-called 'guests' are paying very substantial fees.

Short-term Letting

One fact stands out regarding the short-term let: *every visitor must be supervised*. On one hand he will not know the boundaries, nor where it is safe to shoot; on the other, he will want as good a trophy and as many of them as possible regardless of the rules of good management, or the sport of other clients later in the season.

The owner may feel that he wishes to spread the available sport among as many clients as possible – hotel stalking comes into this category – or stalking may only be possible for very limited periods in the year. In this case the five-day let or some variation can be considered.

Stalking by the day should be avoided if possible. The pleasure of woodland stalking is not measured by the number of deer shot, and particularly not by the size of their antlers. Time is needed to relax and to take in the multitude of scents, sounds and impressions which are enjoyable and memorable in themselves and to which the excitement of the stalk should be added. An extreme case was that of a London business man who drove to the north one Friday afternoon, shot a good stag within an hour of arriving, and was back in town that night. What memories would his trophy conjure up but endless miles of motorway, and maybe a very large bill?

Woodland stalking is, in addition, difficult, and the weather uncertain. Several days may be needed to achieve success, and how much better to have one happy client with a good buck after three days' hard work, than one successful client and two more unsuccessful and discontented? Lastly, each client requires about the same amount of administrative work, whether he comes for one day or several weeks.

If many visitors are to be accommodated, the number will be limited by the number of adult males on the shooting plan and the amount each stalker is allowed, or is capable of shooting. Very few visitors will bother with the necessary tally of young deer. Where a real attempt is being made to manage the deer intensively and the cull of mature bucks approximates to the production, the entire shooting plan should not be offered. Otherwise the last client of the season will be looking for the last shootable buck. In this difficulty the stalker will have to let him take younger or better beasts which would have been better left. In very large forest areas deer management is not likely to be so precise, but even so, middle-aged males should not be over-exploited.

As far as roe are concerned, far the best time to arrange let stalking is in May and early June, before the cover becomes too thick. If the guests fail to get all their bucks, the stalker can arrange for more clients later on, or shoot them himself. If he spares them early on and they are not accounted for, he will fail to get his quota by the end of the season. Many people want to come during the rut in July and August, but it can be a disappointing time.

Shooting sufficient females of all species is more important and more difficult than shooting males. The days are short, and the weather often appalling. It is work best left to professional stalkers who would be hindered by the presence of a paying guest. If gifted amateurs can be found who are really able to help with this work, they should certainly not be expected to pay much for their services.

It is much more important that the correct number is shot from each sex than to shoot the right or wrong animal. Even a professional can use assistance. Particularly from high seats most guests can be accommodated and relied upon to shoot females and young without supervision.

Administration of Stalking Lets

The point has already been made that short-term clients involve more paper-work. Because they are unfamiliar with the local conditions, someone has to answer a wide variety of quite reasonable questions, as well as dealing with hotel reservations, applications for Firearms Certificates, language difficulties, the preparation of bills – often at weekends – and many other trivial items which can make or mar a stalking holiday. One way of passing on many of the difficulties of letting stalking is to leave everything to a sporting agent. All the owner is then expected to do is to lay on the best sport he can, and arrange for a stalker to accompany the guest. He will have to pay the agent a proportion of the revenue and leave the choice of client more or less to his discretion. Problems have occurred with sporting agents based on the Continent because they cannot deal with day-to-day problems, and on occasions have been found to put such a large mark-up on the price charged by the estate that the visitor feels entitled to a better class of sport than was originally intended.

For those wishing to let roe stalking by the week, a set of draft terms and conditions are given in the Reference Section. Each client must be quite clear before he arrives what is the basis of charging. He must pay a substantial fee on acceptance of the booking, otherwise cancellations will wreck the operation, and if at all possible he must be able to take his trophies away with him, after paying the balance.

For this reason, payment for trophies is by skull weight up to Gold Medal standard, where the trophy fees are scaled according to the C.I.C. formula. Trophies of this standard are exceptional, and they should be retained for a photographic record to be made, and then sent to The British Deer Society for measurement. This organisation also issues commemorative medals which are much appreciated by overseas visitors.

Returns Possible

The number of deer which an area of woodland is capable of producing clearly must vary with the habitat. Breeding herds of all the large deer species will produce an annual surplus of about 30 per cent in woodland as opposed to the open hill. Only roe are likely to be considered as a function of deer per hectare, and census-taking is a matter of speculation. Some figures are available for the northern forests, e.g. at Eskdalemuir (12,000 hectares [30,000 acres]) the annual sustained cull in a poor upland area was 500 roe by 1981, while Tabbush gives an average figure for the Forestry Commission's Kielder District between 1971 and 1978 as 738 roe from 39,000 hectares (96,000 acres)[36] though this is more likely to represent the achievements of the ranger staff rather than the maximum yield. On richer land, densities of one roe to four hectares (one to ten acres) are common, and a return of one roe from ten hectares (one from 25 acres) annually could be taken as a reasonable basis for trial.

The average letting value of a good quality mature roebuck is now roughly equivalent to that of a hill stag. Prices for fallow are rather less. While very few woodland stags are yet on offer, weights and trophy size are much in excess of the hill stag, and substantial fees will apply to the largest specimens. Individual trophy charges are normal for red, fallow and sika, and for roe let by the day or week. Block lets will take the overall trophy quality into consideration when calculating the rent.

The larger deer species will be let on a slightly different system, though the same considerations apply. Prices must be clear and the basis precise. If possible an overall charge is better than an hourly charge which makes each unforgiving minute measurable in sterling expended, rather than in memories stored. The client will want to take his trophies home with him. The estate wants to be paid in full before he disappears. A rate per day plus a charge *per capita* is sufficient where the sport is more important than the trophy quality, as with average Highland stags. Otherwise a simple weight or length + beam table can be worked out by taking a selection of local heads, dividing them into groups according to subjective judgment of their value as trophies and then devising a system of measurements which reflects that judgment. Red deer charges based on the number of points per antler can be grossly unfair, while this system cannot be used in any case for fallow or sika. Because of its complexity and the delay likely, the C.I.C. formula should only be used for assessing fees for quite exceptional heads. Besides this, there is always the risk that subsequent measurement in the client's home country may throw up a lower score, and lead to dissatisfaction and disputes.

The best way of recruiting clients is by personal recommendation by existing and approved visitors. Such recommendations should be accepted on the basis that the existing client risks his own sport, should those he recommends fail to measure up to the necessary standards.

Keeping Records

Careful records must be kept each year, not only for the purpose of good management, but to demonstrate to future intending lessees that the deer are not over-exploited, and that trophies of a certain quality have been produced regularly in the past. Every visitor will take away the heads he shoots, and unless measurements and photographs are taken, nothing will remain. Specimen pages for simple but comprehensive records are shown in the Reference Section.

The Organisation of Bookings

Clients, preferably with valid hunting licences from their own country, must be sought and arrangements made at least six months before the stalking season. This will probably be before the full total of the shooting plan is known but clients have to plan their holidays and arrangements for hotels and firearms certificates need to be made many months in advance. If possible, satisfactory clients should be offered provisional options for the following year when they leave.

Timing

The stalking of large deer may necessarily be concentrated about the period of the rut. Visitors for roe stalking are better accommodated earlier in the season as far as possible, as has been explained. Taking clients out, particularly dealing with two at a time, is both time-consuming and a considerable strain on the stalker who should be given a break of a week from time to time in a long series of five-day licences.

Weapons

Visitors Firearms Permits may now be applied for by the host and last for up to one year. In addition to the legal requirements for deer rifles, which vary between England, Wales and Scotland, experience suggests that visitors should be obliged to use a calibre giving over 2200ft/lb muzzle energy for sika stags and over 2500ft/lb muzzle energy for the very large woodland stags found in certain parts of England.

Hotels

Small hotels and guest houses are most likely to be able to adapt to the special demands of stalkers, particularly in the roe season, but newcomers to the trade need to be warned what is required of them in the way of late breakfasts and early dinners, and comings and goings in the small hours. From the client's point of view the rooms need to be quiet so that he can sleep during the day. Accommodation needs to be arranged as close as possible to the forest.

If a zeroing session is insisted upon – as it should be – then stalking on Monday morning is unlikely to be possible and this should be made clear in the literature, as should the possibility, or otherwise, of stalking on Saturdays.

As soon as firm bookings have been arranged everyone likely to be affected, forester, farm manager, factor and stalker is supplied with a list.

Invoicing

Normally the licence fee is payable on acceptance and an invoice should be sent immediately the booking is made. Trophy fees are collected at the end of the week.

Notes for the Stalker

The stalker is, ultimately, the man responsible for the smooth running of commercial stalking, and the enjoyment of his clients during their stay.

These notes are intended to help stalkers who have not much experience of entertaining guests.

Before arrival make sure that everyone knows that you will have a paying guest, and more or less where you will be taking him. Make sure that his Firearms Certificate has been dealt with and that hotel bookings are made and confirmed.

On arrival, try to be at the hotel to make him welcome and discuss plans. Be sure that any rendezvous you make is one that a visitor can find without difficulty, probably in the dark. Have maps of the locality and of the stalking ground. Past records and photographs will be of great interest.

If your guest is a foreigner, take him to the nearest Post Office for a Game Licence which he will almost certainly not have. English people should have one, but may not.

If you are not sure of your man, insist politely on a zeroing session. Clients need firm but tactful handling.

It will assist you to maintain your authority over your guests if you are well turned out.

Try to offer the type of sport the visitor likes. Some like to walk, others to sit in seats, particularly in the evening. The elderly and unfit need special consideration.

Try to vary the locations unless the visitor is particularly set on one individual beast.

Keep up to date with head boiling. When the visitor leaves he will want to take everything possible with him in a presentable state. Ask him if he likes the whole skull, long nose or short nose. Get him to cut his own skulls if possible or at least be present when you cut them. When skulls have been cleaned and bleached in peroxide they should be labelled with full details of shooter, date, time, place, age and trophy size and photographed. The full jawbone should be retained and attached to the trophy.

Keep a note of outings with your client morning and evening, with place, animals shot or missed and other details which will become blurred by the end of the week.

Have your own copy of the price list he has agreed to and measure or weigh the trophies in his presence, giving him the benefit of any doubt. Roe heads charged on a weight scale are weighed 24 hours after boiling with a spring balance calibrated in grammes. In case of doubt the local Post Office will have an accurate machine. If the client wants his roe trophy measured by the British Deer Society in the hope that it will qualify for a medal, anything above the following weights is likely to be in the running for a bronze or better.

	Roe
Full skull (less lower jaw)	430g
Long nose (upper teeth sawn off)	390g
Standard cut (through eye sockets)	340g

Trophies to be sent through the post should be packed in crumpled newspaper in a box which is amply large to take the normal buffeting of parcel post without damage to the delicate skull bones.

Before departure make sure that nothing has been left behind in your transport or at the hotel; see that the client's trophies are well presented and neatly packed for him. Ask if he wants to come again, and if so, when. This is a great help in planning for next season. Regulars should get first chance if they have been satisfactory clients.

In general, remember that what to you is a working week is a special and expensive holiday to the client, and what to you may seem a run-of-the-mill trophy may be to him the event of a lifetime. Make sure that you have allowed him sufficient time for photography before skinning and boiling out the trophy and packing it up before departure.

13 *Problems Affecting Certain Species*

Red Deer

The density of red deer accepted as normal on the open hill can never be tolerated in productive woodland, nor will they behave in the same way once they are established in the forest. Even in the rut, small groups can be expected consisting of half a dozen hinds and followers accompanied by a stag. There will be little or nothing of the constant activity traditional to Highland conditions, and roaring will mostly be restricted to a short period morning and evening, particularly when the weather is clear and frosty.

Because the groups are small, they will find sufficient browse in a restricted area, and unless the forest is devoid of food, large aggregations of deer are unlikely. The system of forest design advocated where a large number of small control and feeding areas are scattered through each forest block will ensure that the deer do not need to travel long distances to farm crops or vulnerable plantations. If disturbance is kept to a minimum they will adopt a diurnal feeding habit which facilitates control, and avoids excessive peeling damage.

In spite of the enormous lengths of deer fencing erected in Scotland – 3000 miles (4830km) up to 1979[37] – and an annual erection and maintenance bill in excess of £500,000, few fenced areas will remain deer-proof for more than a decade after planting, and one can safely predict that most forested land from Caithness to the English side of the border will be holding a resident population of red deer by the end of the century. The majority will be colonised long before.[38]

If provision for controlling this vast future red deer herd is not built into the present forestry plan, no amount of palliative actions such as night shooting or round-the-year action regardless of humanitarian considerations will be sufficient. One has only to look to New Zealand, where bounty hunting, mass killing from aircraft and distribution of poisoned bait all failed to produce a complete kill, though the forest cover is by no means as continuous as in a typical Scottish sitka forest.

A new generation of stalkers will have to bring the profession of woodland stalking to as high a pitch as their fathers have done on the hill. The two have little in common. *To do this, they will need the active and sympathetic collaboration of every forester, if the principal aim of deer management, the reduction of damage, is to be achieved.*

Although the current fencing of wintering grounds is adversely affecting the well-being of red deer in many parts of Scotland, the effect is transitory and completely dependent on the maintenance in perpetuity of many miles of deer fence. Once the deer have the advantage of access to the forest, they will profit by the shelter and food thus provided to increase in body weight and in antler size. Although numbers will have to be kept much lower than on the open hill, the deer will still represent a substantial asset, especially where forest and hill land are managed together. The high ground will then support many deer through the summer and offer traditional hill stalking enhanced in value by greater trophy size and weight of venison.

The greatest problems are now being encountered where forests laid out without regard for deer control have reached the stage of production and replanting. The measures that can be adopted in such cases tend to be expensive – such as internal fencing – or inhumane – such as out-of-season or night shooting. In the long run these expedients are unlikely to prove cost-effective. Deer soon learn, stalkers become sickened and disillusioned by the duties imposed on them, and public distaste will quickly bring forestry into disrepute. The present problems are acknowledged; we must ensure that they are not perpetuated in the second rotation.

Fallow Deer

Like red deer, fallow have their seasonal movement patterns, congregating at traditional stands for the rut in late September and October, but dispersing later in the year in response to the availability of food.[39] They have also a marked response to daily temperature changes, resulting in movement up and down hill. Their habit of wandering over a large area rather like the circuit of a man-eating tiger, is, however, difficult to predict. Fallow have been known to disappear from a wood, only to reappear in similar numbers a year or more later, or to desert an area completely if the habitat is changed, for example by clear-felling or constant disturbance.

They are by preference animals of pole stage and semi-mature woodland. A wood which has been completely felled and replanted may be uninhabited by fallow for several years until the thickets become hollow once again, when they are likely to recolonise it, replacing the roe or muntjac which may have been profiting from the thick cover in the meanwhile.

Being largely grazing animals, fallow can be an agricultural pest. Their travels to and from the fields lead to well-marked paths and racks developing, which should be noted by the stalker and recorded on a large-scale map. In areas where the deer are of different colours, details can be built up of numbers and movements by observing the colour-combinations of the different parties.

Large groups of does and juveniles may be encountered, causing understandable complaints. If one is shot *and the stalker immediately shows himself to the deer* the surprise may be enough to drive the whole herd away long enough for the crop to grow up, or to be harvested. If not, it may be necessary to identify and shoot the lead doe.

Alternative crops for the deer can help to minimise complaints by farmers but, as discussed in Chapter 8, they must be more succulent and better fertilised than the crops one wishes to draw them off.

In the spring most agricultural crops receive one or a number of chemical applications, fertiliser or pesticide and nearly all of these are sufficient to deter fallow completely for quite a time. Once cereals or grass have grown to a height of 10cm (4in) deer will tend to leave them in any case.

Fallow can be a pest just before harvest because they like to lie up in the corn. One or two portable high seats may be needed to see them or get a clear shot. Surprisingly few corn stalks in the line of flight are needed to divert a bullet, or make it break up.

Sika

The fact that sika and red deer can inter-breed to produce fertile hybrids has caused a great deal of unease in some traditional red deer areas which sika are colonising, such as Eire, Lancashire and Inverness-shire.[40]

The question is, under what circumstances do these hybrids arise? Are they inevitable where red and sika share the same habitat or is there some inter-specific barrier which prevents the mesalliance in normal circumstances? Experience in Melbury Park where red and sika have existed side by side for a hundred years without hybridisation suggests the latter. Even where the two species are in full rut on the same 20-acre bowl of turf, one seems to take no notice whatever of the other.

In the revised (1982) edition of the B.D.S. publication *Sika Deer*[41] the authors quote work by Lowe and Gardiner which casts doubt on the accepted taxonomy of sika. They suggest that whereas the Japanese race of *Cervus n. nippon* and *C. n. keramae* are acceptable sub-species, the mainland races *hortulorum*, *manchuricus* and *kopschi* and the Formosan race *tiaouanus* appear to be synonymous.

It seems that hybridization in the wild as opposed to park conditions is only between red deer and Manchurian sika and that where Japanese sika and red deer have been inhabiting the same area they appear to be reproductively isolated. For example in Killarney (South west Ireland) they have shared the same range since the Nineteenth Century and no hybrids have appeared. Certain facts have emerged from this investigation which seem to indicate that some if not all of the sub-species of sika deer may be entirely of hybrid origin:

1   Hinds from the same species from the mainland hybridize freely with red deer while the Japanese sika do not.

2   Hybrids between Japanese sika stags and red deer hinds in the F.2 and subsequent generations produce individuals which are indistinguishable from the mainland and Formosan forms.

This suggests to us that the latter may well be the products of hybridization between Japanese sika and Chinese wapiti bred (selectively perhaps?) in the distant past in Chinese parks from which they subsequently escaped or were released as has happened more recently in Britain and Ireland. If this hypothesis is correct it follows that the mainland and Formosan forms cannot be classified as belonging to any species, let alone to be con-specific with sika deer, the latter being confined in its distribution to the Japanese islands.

This leads to the conclusion that hybridisation is only likely between Manchurian sika and red deer in normal conditions in the wild, but that mating between Japanese sika and red deer might arise under conditions of extreme stress where constant disturbance, for example, in an effort to control forest damage, or over-exploitation of the deer population leaves a few in-season red hinds without an attendant stag.

It appears from all available evidence that although sika are colonising large parts of the Scottish Highlands they do not, on the whole, occupy the same niche as red deer, preferring the scrubby fringes of the moor.

Sika in this country have not so far been blamed for a great deal of forest damage,[42] although problems have cropped up abroad, notably in Denmark. In the New Forest sika stags have the habit of prodding the boles of large conifers and damaging them, but on the whole their preference for grazing brings them into conflict more with farmers than with foresters. They tend to be more nocturnal than red or fallow deer.[43]

A stalker having the misfortune to wound a sika stag has a problem on his hands: they are adept at hiding and will lie in a hollow or forestry furrow without moving until actually trodden on. The other point which should not be forgotten is that wounded sika can turn on the stalker or his dog, and even an apparently dead stag should always be treated with prudence, in case it is merely stunned or lightly wounded.

A larger rifle than might be suggested by their size is recommended for sika. Although the professional stalker will find the .243 Winchester quite satisfactory, a visitor is well advised to arm himself with something heavier, especially for the stags, to avoid these problems.

Roe Deer

Although the damage that roe do is mostly limited to the first five years or so after planting, browsing during this time can increase materially establishment costs, or even check the crop completely. They are capable of finding places to live even when the undergrowth of a large conifer block is mostly killed out, and numbers of roe build up unobtrusively to a density which is only appreciated when new plantations are made, and severe damage results.

Control must continue, and be made easy, throughout the rotation.

Perhaps more than any other deer species, the roe attracts the overseas enthusiast who can be very convincing on the perfections of roe management as practised in his home country. A massive literature also exists, principally, but not exclusively, in German. The problem is that while we should be able to draw on this fund of knowledge to improve our own roe management, much accepted tradition is either fallacious, or is based on conditions which are totally different from our own. Possibly as a consequence, two apparently opposed schools of thought on roe management seem to be evolving in this country: the selective shooting, 'Master Buck' protagonists, and those who suggest that all one can do is to exploit the venison potential by culling. Study of the foregoing sections of this book should make it clear that any scheme of management has to be related to the scale of operations. A few acres of Sussex woodland can be managed intensively, while large forestry blocks in the North need more empirical methods. In either case, however, too high a density, an uneven sex ratio or over-exploitation of the middle-aged bucks are equally undesirable.

While the techniques and theory of roe management have been set out elsewhere, the basic rules for culling can be summarised. Instead of the selection by antler quality so widely advocated, bucks should be divided into rough age classes: young, middle-aged and old, and the cull should be divided in the proportion of 60, 20 and 20 per cent. Does should be shot without selection. A slightly higher number of does shot than bucks is needed to keep the balance.[44]

Attempts to count roe are notably unreliable, and shooting plans should be gradually increased year by year until there is a noticeable effect on numbers. Nothing is worse than too high a density, both from the point of view of preserving antler quality and preventing damage. Low body weights in comparison with neighbouring areas usually indicate an over-population.

Muntjac

These small deer have spread throughout the English midlands since they escaped from Woburn Park before the Second World War. Their size and preference for very thick cover makes control difficult and large populations have built up in suitable woodlands, often without the owners becoming aware of them.

Muntjac can be readily distinguished from roe by their short legs and rounded back, and the possession of a large tail, which is sometimes carried erect in flight. Chinese Water deer, which also exist locally in the wild, have been confused with muntjac. They are more lightly constructed, have only a short dark tail, and the hind legs are noticeably longer than the forelegs. Roebucks have comparatively long antlers on short pedicles, muntjac have short antlers on long furry pedicles, and Chinese Water deer have no antlers at all. Both the latter species have long tushes in the upper jaw.

Muntjac can do considerable damage to tender young trees, and to Nature Conservation and game shooting interests by destruction of the herb and shrub layer. In spite of their build, they are capable of jumping surprisingly high fences, especially when pursued. Many muntjac are killed on the roads, and others are taken by dogs, but such natural losses are not sufficient to limit numbers. They are not seasonal breeders, one offspring being produced every seven months. Control techniques have not yet been evolved completely, but the winter and early spring is the best time to come to terms with them. Stalking, moving and netting (for which a licence is required) are all successful. Possibly the most promising seems to be sitting up over a favoured spot, which can be baited with grain, fruit, etc., or crop patches can be grown for the purpose.

Muntjac have thick skins, and the use of shotguns is to be deprecated. (Under the Wildlife & Countryside Act the shotgun is outlawed except under certain stringent conditions.) The same legal requirements for rifles apply to muntjac as to all other deer.

Chinese Water Deer

This species is not widely distributed, although scattered colonies are being discovered which have been mistakenly identified as muntjac.[45] They are slightly taller at the shoulder (males 50–54cm [20–21in]) compared to muntjac (males 43–46cm [17–18in]) and both sexes are without antlers. Chinese water deer have not been blamed for much damage, though they could possibly be a nuisance to market gardeners. Small saplings are scraped by the bucks in November and December as part of their rutting activity. Lawrence gives the maximum diameter as 12mm ($\frac{1}{2}$in) and states that the bark is not normally ruptured, though the trees are polished by the teeth.[46] Very young coppice growth may be browsed. Multiple births are normal, an average of 2.3 fawns being quoted, though with a high natural mortality. At present these deer do not appear to present any major problem.

Interactions between Deer Species

Red and sika deer are the only two species wild in the U.K. which are near enough genetically to interbreed, though other deer related both to red and sika exist in zoos and parks. Siberian roe, which existed in the vicinity of Woburn Park from 1910 to about 1950 would probably have been capable of mating with our native stock. During the period there could have been no contact in that area as the nearest roe population was at Thetford in Norfolk. According to Whitehead, the colony has long died out.[47]

There appears to be little antipathy between red and roe deer, in fact a form of 'fagging' has been noted between a stag and a roebuck, while fallow deer are not commonly seen in close association with other species in the wild.[48] The main interaction concerns the availability of browse. If red or fallow deer are present in large numbers, not only will the ground vegetation be used up, but a marked browse line will develop at a height the roe cannot reach. Thus the type of habitat is changed from thick low cover to open floor, but winter food is denied to the smaller species. It follows that if roe are the preferred species, red or fallow deer must be prevented from becoming too numerous.

Sika appear to have fairly precise habitat requirements which set them apart from other deer to some extent, though undoubtedly they do share some land with either red deer or roe, or both. In south Dorset where a substantial herd exists in the neighbourhood of Poole Harbour, their preference seems to be for the low-lying acid sands of Wareham Heath, much of which now carries pine plantations. Stragglers from this herd are found from time to time on the surrounding chalk downlands, but very dry country does not seem congenial to them. In red deer country they usually inhabit plantations and scrubland on the edge of the moor, rather than the open hill.

When muntjac colonised the Midlands they found a vacant ecological niche in the absence of roe deer. Recently they have started to share the same woods with roe, but the consequences have not yet become apparent. They do share the same habitat preferences, and to some extent the same food, so a degree of competition is likely. While replacement of roe to any degree by muntjac is undesirable from the sporting point of view, some increase in browsing damage by roe is also possible as the muntjac population builds up and some of the available feed is used by them.

Domestic Stock and Deer

Deer movements are profoundly affected by the presence of domestic stock in their use of fields for feeding, in their reactions to disturbance by shepherds etc., and as a response to the presence of stock in the woods.

Cattle on the whole are treated with a certain prudent reserve, but deer may continue to graze fields after cattle have been turned in. Sheep, in contrast, are anathema to them and only hunger will drive deer to share a field with sheep, or to return to a crop for a time after a flock has been removed. This is due to the fouled ground which roe in particular do not enjoy.

A change in farming policy from cattle to sheep can have fundamental effects, not only on deer movement, but as a consequence of this, on the woodland habitat and ultimately on forest damage. To give an instance of this chain of events, a well-wooded estate in Dorset changed from beef cattle to intensive sheep farming. Some of the woods were cleared, and sheep fences were erected round all the fields. Between the physical barriers, dislike of sheep and the greater disturbance needed to look after them, fallow deer were no longer seen feeding by day in the fields. Being forced to live in the woods, the herd proved too large for the available browse and everything within reach was soon eaten. The effect of this was to make the woods cold and draughty so that they would no longer hold pheasants, previously a valuable asset on the estate. Then the deer, being both hungry and unable to range, set about a large beech plantation, creating very severe damage by stripping the bark.

More direct, and even more disastrous to the deer is the practice common in the north of Scotland of wintering stock, either sheep or cattle, in woodland. The effect on the habitat is to destroy all the understory. If the stocking is heavy the trampling and dung deposited changes the soil characteristics so that the natural ground vegetation is replaced the following spring by a wilderness of nettles. This is likely to make the woods unsuitable for recolonisation even when the stock has been removed. Recent work by the Forestry Commission has shown that over-wintering stock in plantations also has some adverse effects on the crop.[49]

In spite of this, having warm lying for stock in the winter has obvious advantages under some conditions. If a reasonably large area of wood is available, it is suggested that they are restricted to some part of it, so that the consequences to the environment are not so universal.

14 *Poaching and its Suppression*

Attitudes towards Poaching

Anyone with the responsibility of defending property of any sort may quite reasonably feel that the law is more concerned with protecting the rights of the lawbreaker. Also that the courts are rarely inclined to take a serious view of poaching, compared for example to driving a motor car above the permitted speed or other major crime. In a recent debate in the House of Lords the case was quoted by Lord Burton[50] of a poacher who fired five shots at a stag with a .22 rifle, failing incidentally to kill it. He was fined £10 for having a rifle without a certificate, £5 for shooting out of season, £5 for shooting a stag without permission, a total of £20 for fatally injuring an animal worth over £100. No account was taken of the cruelty involved.

The main problem is, after all, to catch the perpetrator without suffering physical violence and to get him into court with a reasonable case to answer. If, perhaps after months of work, the case is dismissed with a derisory fine, everyone concerned is left with a feeling of bitterness and frustration.

Certain steps have recently been taken to set matters right. A summary of current law affecting deer is given in the Reference Section. The Deer Act 1980 made trespass in pursuit of deer an offence in England and Wales for the first time. Penalties have also been brought up to date, and the powers of the police to stop, search and arrest have been much strengthened. A constable may now enter on land if he suspects an offence has been committed, instead of being forced to wait patiently on the nearest highway.

The traffic in poached venison has been hampered by making the sale of venison other than to a licensed game or venison dealer an offence, and by obliging the dealer to keep records of the origin of all venison he purchases. Similar legislation affecting penalties and the regulation of game dealers in Scotland is covered by the provisions of the Deer (Scotland) (Amendment) Act 1982, which is summarised in the Reference Section.

It remains for landowners and stalkers to improve their techniques for catching poachers, to develop relations with the local police force so that assistance is at hand; to see that a full list of charges is preferred, and not least to persuade Magistrates and Sheriffs to view the current wave of poaching in the correct perspective.

There can be no doubt that poaching is now highly profitable and highly organised. Radio is extensively used, large lurchers are being bred for the business and freely advertised in some journals. The degree to which violence is expected can be judged by the large majority of gamekeepers who now regard an alsatian or dobermann as essential not only to protect themselves when on patrol but often their families as well. In addition to game and deer, farm stock is also being taken from the fields. These are frequently gutted and skinned on the spot to get rid of any identifying marks.

Large-scale poaching of deer can demolish any plans for logical management, and make letting (a major asset on many estates) virtually impossible. The value of a deer in any normal poaching case is usually given as so many pounds' worth of venison. This takes no account of its trophy value, or the replacement cost. In this instance we should follow the continental practice of valuing a poached deer at the cost of purchasing an equivalent one alive. In the case of a large stag this might represent thousands rather than hundreds of pounds, but the argument is a fair one.

Suppression

Alarms

In the age of micro-electronics, the development of cheap and efficient intruder alarms should not be difficult, although various mechanical problems have to be overcome. Basically the trigger of an alarm system is an interrupted electric current. A straightforward loop circuit of breakable wire is satisfactory round a pheasant pen, for example. Pressure pads or infra-red or micro-wave beams are effective where no deer are present. The problem is that the size and weight of deer make them difficult to distinguish from men by these means. Two alternatives are being developed: the audio detector unit programmed to react to the response frequencies of rifle or shotgun discharge acoustics, and the metal detector unit.

Once the trigger has been activated, the signal can be used to activate a variety of alarm devices depending on suitability and budget. Sirens are the cheapest, and can be quite effective. If the man responsible is at a distance, radio links are more reliable than land lines to sound an alarm at his house. In the case of multiple lay-outs warning lights indicate which circuit has been triggered. The most sophisticated units can be set to dial a series of pre-set telephone numbers until one is answered.

Probably the most effective weapon is portable radio, with a pre-arranged link-up between estates, so that help can be summoned and the police alerted. Night vision equipment, at present expensive or restricted to the services, should soon be available. It is almost certainly already being used by poachers.

The law (*see also* Reference Section)
Arrest and seizure of suspected poachers and their equipment should be left if possible to the police. The powers of owners and their employees vary widely according to the offence, but are in general restricted to taking names and addresses, and escorting the poacher to the nearest road. In addition any attempt to arrest or seize equipment may provoke violence.

A scheme which in the long run is more likely to lead to the suppression of poaching was launched recently in the West Midlands. The procedure was as follows: various landowners arranged a meeting with the Chief Constable to discuss poaching in the area. After this a fairly open meeting was called at which the matter was handed over to the Crime Prevention Officer of the Gloucestershire Constabulary. Selected keepers, owners and a local game dealer met the police of the various divisions in Gloucestershire. Good liaison having been established, regular meetings take place at divisional level between the police and invited keepers. At these small meetings one principal co-ordinating keeper and one other represent the owners, and one or two sergeants the police – although other more senior police officers often drop in. There is now a better understanding by rural people of how the police work. When there is an incident to report they quote the relevant police map and rendezvous numbers which speeds the response of the police. The police have become very keen and the word has gone round the poaching community that Gloucestershire is no longer good news.

At police headquarters level, two meetings per year are held and there is a free interchange of information with adjoining forces. Local people connected with the scheme have been enthusiastic over the response from the police in interest and involvement, as well as the effect the scheme has had on poaching and crime locally.

The police are also now in the position of being able to inspect venison dealers' records. If they feel that the landowners are collaborating to the best of their ability and a good relationship has been built up, they are likely to respond to a quiet word on any suspicions of illicit dealing. The same relationship will allow suggestions to be made when a poacher is arrested about additional charges which might be brought against him. Poachers are notorious for their intimate knowledge of the law. Their opponents should also have specialist knowledge which they can bring to the attention of the police at that very important moment.

Man traps

Man traps were banned in the last century, but a recent case was brought concerning a 'bed of nails' which was placed in a ditch to deter a poacher who was in the habit of crawling up it. The poacher accused the owner of setting a man trap and won his case, which makes it clear that sundry devices should not be placed in any position where they could cause injury. However, farm implements can quite properly be left about the countryside and if a poacher drives his car over a forgotten harrow, he has only himself to blame. The owner should not, however, fail to remember it himself, or to remind his farm men. Otherwise the cost in tractor tyres will go a long way in paying for a better anti-poaching device.

15 *Local Control and Management Societies*

History of Management Societies

Deer are no respecters of man-made boundaries and a dialogue between neighbours is obviously needed where a herd of deer, or elements of it, wander at will between two estates. They may harbour on one but feed on the other, or winter on one and rut on the other. Logical management demands some form of collaboration.

The idea of forming local Deer Control Societies developed after the Second World War in the south-east of England. As more societies were formed, their ideals and structure changed in accordance with the conditions in each area.

The pioneers were largely stalkers who combined with more progressive and humane landowners in an attempt to stamp out the shotgunning and snaring of deer which were then considered normal, also to introduce rifle shooting as the proper alternative. Because many of the holdings in the south-east are small and the deer, especially fallow, liable to move arbitrarily from one farm to another, the organisation of the first societies had the nature of a police force, stalkers being ready to respond to calls for help with rapid action. Deer were regarded as a pest, having little value, and the stalkers gave their time as a service to the farmers.

In the 1960s the stalking of roe deer slowly became more valuable and a new type of control society, or more properly, management society came into being. These concentrated more on developing and unifying the management of a deer community. Where estates contained enough woodland, each would retain a stalker, amateur or professional, or one stalker would look after a group of smaller properties. The 'police force' aspect remained for odd complaints, usually from gardens. This development allowed some estates to let their stalking, while retaining control of deer management through the stalker's attendance at meetings. In marked contrast, the older-established societies founded on the principle that no money should be involved, found their services less in demand as substantial rents began to be offered for stalking. The pioneers, having demonstrated through their devoted work that the new methods could work, were disillusioned when overtaken by commerce.

There is no doubt that local deer management groups do have a beneficial effect in promoting new ideas and preventing to a limited extent the under- or over-exploitation of the deer. Better liaison between estates can also help considerably in the fight against poaching. For some reason the free exchange of information on numbers and distribution seems to become inhibited as the value of venison and stalking increases, which is regrettable.

For many years the British Deer Society has fathered the Deer Control

Societies. Draft rules are published and a useful booklet, *Deer Control and Deer Control Societies*, is obtainable from their headquarters.

In Scotland a different type of management group has evolved in response to the problems posed by the vagrant habits of red deer on the open hill. In many ways the need for concerted action is more apparent than in the south. Red deer, especially the stags, range over miles of hill from one season to another, representing an important asset in one part of the range, and a pest in another. One landowner may harbour a large proportion of the hind population, while the stags summer some distance from where they rut. Changes in land use, for example fencing and planting traditional wintering ground, can reduce the carrying capacity. Taken to excess, or lacking careful design so that all access to low ground is shut off by fences, such a planting programme can literally sterilise thousands of acres of high ground which the deer alone can use. It is in the interests of all owners to manage both deer and their entire range as one unit.

Areas which have been afforested will play a vital part in the future of red deer in Scotland, although it is easy to disregard fenced areas as totally lost to them. There is no way in which those fences will be maintained in perpetuity, so the new forests will act as future lodging for large numbers of red deer, welcome or not. The Forestry Commission, forestry investment companies and private woodland owners need to keep a keen interest and involvement in the overall deer management situation as it changes and stabilises in new patterns.

Management Groups in the Future

In a south country context, the deer management position is changing rapidly as exploitation both legal and illicit reaches the point where the deer population actually starts to be reduced. Anyone involved with roe deer control in the last forty years has learned to assume that an almost limitless reservoir of surplus deer exists over the border, only waiting to re-occupy

any territory left vacant. Strategies of management have taken it for granted, quite rightly, that such was the case. This state of affairs can no longer be assumed to exist anywhere in the south, and a new sensitivity to variations in population density is necessary nowadays if deer stocks are not to be over-exploited. Under these circumstances the deer, at last under control, become a fragile asset, to be conserved in the full meaning of the term. Co-operation between estates is then imperative.

Further north the average size of holdings is larger, and particularly in remote areas the degree of exploitation will be less and the style of management extensive rather than intensive. The function of regional groups will be more in the field of rationalising management, of encouraging information between owners and of developing collaboration between stalkers so that they can develop pride and expertise in the profession of woodland stalking.

Eventually groups throughout the country can be expected to organise poacher protection schemes, combined operations involving teamwork between stalkers on neighbouring ground, joint training courses and co-operative schemes for improving the marketing of venison, deer products and stalking as an integral part of both land use and forest management.

Some of the Major Diseases and Parasites of Deer

A. McDiarmid, D.Sc., Ph.D., M.R.C.V.S.,
F.R.C.Path., F.R.S.E.

From the practical point of view, anything which prevents an animal leading a normal life, e.g. moving, eating, reproducing, etc., may be considered a disease. In recent years, much interest has been shown in metabolic disease of farm animals. This is understandable, as these species are called upon to behave in a totally abnormal manner, e.g. a cow has to produce far more milk than it requires for feeding its own calf, and sheep and pigs are often asked to produce more progeny in a season than hitherto. Deer have none of these difficulties to contend with, but nevertheless suffer from various nutritional disorders according to their habitats. Disease is, however, generally caused either by ecto- or endo-parasites or by a host of micro-organisms ranging from minute viruses to the larger bacteria, protozoa and fungi. It is remarkable how resistant deer are to a very wide range of potential pathogens and the various metabolic disorders which can readily be produced in cattle by nutritional changes. For example, red deer grazing a Scottish mountain do not appear to suffer from braxy in the same way as the sheep in the vicinity.

Apart from a few notable exceptions, the association between deer and their parasites appears to involve a great deal of tolerance between the infective agents and their hosts unless some other extraneous factors intervene, such as bad management, e.g. overstocking, poor nutrition or severe climatic conditions. Thus the disease agents are often present in apparently healthy deer and a breakdown in health occurs when the balance between the host and the parasite is upset. There are many other complicating factors such as the necessity, in some instances, for more than one micro-organism to be present to precipitate a clinical attack and often stress of one kind or another is involved. Sometimes genetic factors are suspected of playing a part, such as in the case of enzootic ataxia in red deer *Cervus elaphus*. This disease, which causes the animal to stagger and eventually lose control of it's hindquarters, is associated with a depressed copper level in the body and is quite common in the United Kingdom. It is remarkable that cases have never been seen in freeliving wild deer, only in those confined in deer parks, where the master stags have every opportunity to mate with their own offspring. This example is given merely to illustrate the complexities of disease in deer and other animals and to emphasise the fact that it is brought about by a mixture of circumstances, many of which are very difficult to identify.

Nutritional Diseases

The most common nutritional disease of deer is general food deficiency. This is especially true in circumstances such as exist in the Scottish Highlands. The report by Cheatum and Severinghaus (1950) demonstrated very clearly that the productivity of a deer herd depends on the availability of food under natural conditions. They examined deer on good and on poor ground and found the latter situation was associated with the production of fewer embryos. In fact, they showed that 10 does on good quality food produced as many fawns as 15 does on poor ground. Maybe the most striking example of this phenomenon concerns the Scottish red deer population where hinds frequently produce a calf in alternative years, although the same species in New Zealand can produce a viable calf per hind every year and sometimes even twins, a situation virtually unknown in Scotland. It is clear that protein deficiency, due for example to overbrowsing, must be at least a contributing factor to poor reproductive performance in deer. Mortality, associated with malnutrition, can be continued with the subsequent fawn crop and, in herds which are very badly managed, this juvenile mortality can be very high, e.g. even 50 per cent. Quite apart from its direct effect, food deficiency can predispose the animals to many diseases and parasitic infestations which, under normal conditions, would probably not affect them clinically. Good management is therefore vital to prevent losses from diseases which are normally subclinical. It must be stressed, however, that good feeding will not control losses from some of the more important highly contagious or infectious diseases, especially those of viral origin, such as Foot and Mouth Disease or Rinderpest.

Sometimes specific mineral deficiencies occur and imbalance of the calcium/phosphorus ratio can visibly affect antler growth, but generally these are not of much importance so far as actual mortality is concerned. Deer, in reasonable numbers, tend to have a far larger selection of browse in most areas than farm stock and hence do not show so much effect from the lack of specific local trace elements as do their domestic counterparts.

Natural Toxicological Factors

Plant poisoning is very rare in deer apart from a few exceptional circumstances. Laurel has been incriminated from time to time. In England, laurel trimmings from a garden, thrown into a deer park and allowed to wilt, were attractive enough to the fallow deer to be responsible for the sudden deaths of several of the best bucks. Yew poisoning can also occur, particularly in a hard winter when browse is scarce or when the tree falls down; fallow deer in the New Forest have died from this cause. On the whole, deer will not eat poisonous plants unless forced to do so. Isolated individual cases of mortality, caused by black nightshade and similar toxic plants, have also been reported in the U.S.A. Acorns when eaten in large quantities in the green state, e.g. in overgrazed deer parks, will cause death in some instances.

Chemical poisoning is uncommon, e.g. arsenic (Hayes *et al.*, 1957). Again, it was overgrazing of the habitat which forced the deer to eat cotton plants which had been previously dusted with arsenic. Other insecticides have sometimes been incriminated but these instances are rare and of little significance in practice. They should, however, be watched carefully for harmful effects in the future when their use might be increased. Fortunately, deer consume a very large variety of foods and not very much of any one substance at any one time; they often eat potentially poisonous plants when they are least toxic. Good herd management with adequate food for the number of animals involved will always act as an effective insurance against possible poisoning.

Viral Diseases

Foot and Mouth Disease (F.M.D.)

Deer can become infected with F.M.D. under natural conditions and as long ago as 1924 there was a serious outbreak in the Stanislaus Forest in California. It was decided to try to control the outbreak by a slaughter policy and 22,000 deer were killed. Ten per cent of these animals showed evidence of past or present clinical disease. Many different species of deer have since been shown to be affected, particularly in Germany, but on the whole deer seem to have played little or no part in the general epidemiology of this condition. In the past, despite many outbreaks of the disease in farm livestock in the United Kingdom and despite the considerable number of different species of deer obviously at risk, no natural cases of this disease have ever been confirmed in deer. Subsequent to the last outbreak of F.M.D. some 14 years ago, it was decided that the susceptibility of British deer should be determined by experimental infection.

Accordingly, samples of the various species were assembled and exposed to infection under controlled conditions at the Animal Virus Research Institute in the United Kingdom. The results were reported by Gibbs *et al.*, (1975) and showed quite clearly that all five species of deer found in the British countryside, namely red, fallow, roe *Capreolus capreolus*, sika *Cervus nippon* and muntjac *Muntiacus reevesi* became infected. The clinical disease was severe in roe and muntjac and some animals actually died from the infection. The disease was less severe in sika and subclinical in red and fallow deer. Transmission from deer to their own species and to cattle was confirmed. The excretion of virus from the affected deer was similar to excretion in sheep and cattle. Some deer became persistent carriers, shedding virus for at least 28 days after infection. There can be no doubt, therefore, that a range of different species of deer are susceptible to a varying degree although, under normal field conditions in Britain, they appear to play no part in the general epidemiology of the disease.

Epizootic Haemorrhagic Disease (E.H.D.)

This acute, highly fatal, virus disease was first reported by Shope *et al.* (1955) in white-tailed deer *Odocoileus virginanus*, in New Jersey. It occurs in several other States as well in the U.S.A. Several distinct serotypes have been described. Mortality can sometimes be very high, e.g. 60 per cent in the 1971 outbreak. After exposure to experimental infection with the virus, the animals exhibit a diphasic febrile reaction in about three to five days; severe congestion of the visible mucous membranes and the eye is sometimes followed by bleeding. Death often ensues rather rapidly, within a day or two. On post mortem examination, there are visible and microscopic haemorrhages in virtually every tissue of the body and often considerable oedema. So far, there is no evidence of successful transmission to other species apart from deer. The deer themselves show considerable variation in susceptibility. The disease may, in fact, have been present in the endemic areas for a considerable time and Shope *et al.* (1960) suggested that 'Black Tongue' was in all probability E.H.D. The white-tailed deer seem particularly susceptible and details of experimental transmission to this species are available from the paper by Jones *et al.* (1977), who also pointed out that *Culicoides variipennis* was the vector of E.H.D. virus. Recently, Gibbs *et al.*, (1977) pointed out the close similarity of this agent to Blue Tongue virus, and showed that E.H.D. virus injected experimentally into British red, fallow and roe deer failed to produce any clinical disease, although viraemia occurred in all three species. They also showed that the maximum titres associated with the viraemia were higher in cattle, sheep and muntjac deer.

Blue Tongue (B.T.V.)
Although closely allied to E.H.D. this viral disease does not appear to cause much trouble in deer. Thomas and Prestwood (1976) showed that many white-tailed deer were positive to antibody tests for the virus but clinical disease does not apparently ensue subsequent to infections. More evidence is provided by Hoff and others (1974) and white-tailed deer in Texas showed an antibody response of the order of 89 per cent. The disease has also been experimentally transmitted to elk *Cervus Canadensis* (Murray and Trainer, 1970), showing that the animals were susceptible, antibody being detected in two weeks although clinical signs were mild.

In its natural hosts, B.T.V. does not appear to be of much consequence. The main problem is how the virus might react with a new, hitherto unknown cervine host.

Rinderpest
Although this has always been a very important viral infection of cattle and big game animals in Africa and the Middle and Far East, the disease has never reached North America. Outbreaks have occurred in several species of deer in zoological collections in Europe and in India and Gupta and Verma (1949), describing such an outbreak at the Calcutta zoo, suggested it might have originated from fodder brought from an area where cattle were already infected. The mortality rate in the deer was 61 per cent but the virus was not isolated although the clinical signs were considered good enough presumptive evidence. Vaccination against this disease was eventually so successful that in some instances a false sense of security was created and this resulted in a pandemic across the Middle East from Afghanistan to the Mediterranean. Despite the severity of this outbreak, no species of wild life seemed to be implicated. This very serious outbreak was eventually halted by vaccination and stringent quarantine regulations.

All the natural hosts for this virus are in the Order Artiodactyla and the check list by Curasson (1932) has recently been updated by Scott (1976). There is great variation between the species in their reaction to the virus but this disease must be considered as one of the most serious potential infections of the cervids. Some recent experimental work by Hamby and others (1975) showed that white-tailed deer were very susceptible, death occurring in five to six days after exposure to the virus.

Malignant Catarrh (M.C.E.)
This infection, due to a fragile virus, is obviously of considerable importance so far as deer are concerned. Originally it was reported in African

buffaloes, which were considered to be the main reservoir hosts, but sheep are now considered to be of even greater significance, little or no clinical disease appearing in them although they are a potent source of virus. One of the most interesting outbreaks ever recorded in deer occurred in the Père David deer *E. davidianus* at Whipsnade Zoo (Huck *et al.*, 1961). The infection was readily transmitted to experimental red deer and one of the interesting features was the long incubation period of up to 48 days. The disease then had a sudden onset, the animals were very dull and had a muco-purulent discharge from the eyes and nose with considerable salivation. The source of the infection was never adequately explained. Quite recently another small outbreak occurred in Scotland in a small group of red deer which had been moved into a paddock recently vacated by sheep. Sanford *et al.*, (1977) described the condition in detail. The first U.S.A. report concerned Axis deer *Axis axis* followed by other reports in white-tailed deer and mule deer *O. hemionus*. Cases in sika were also recorded, in which the deer had been in close contact with sheep. It appears that this disease is of considerable significance, as a wide range of deer species appear to be susceptible and its prevention is rendered difficult by the presence of virus in symptomless carriers and hitherto unknown natural hosts.

Mucosal disease
Richards and others (1956) have given a good description of this disease in white-tailed deer and mule deer in North Dakota. Apparently it has been transmitted both ways using bacteria-free blood and tissue suspensions. The clinical signs are weakness, lack of sensitivity, dehydration and emaciation; the faeces contain stringy mucus and drops of blood. Post mortem examination reveals much the same picture as in cattle, viz. erosions and ulcerations of the alimentary tract, but deer do not show the encrustations on the muzzle and there are no erosions of the oral cavity. In many ways the clinical syndrome is similar to E.H.D. but differs mainly in the fact that it is readily transmitted to cattle. Nevertheless, there is still considerable confusion in differential diagnosis.

Vesicular Stomatitis (V.S.V.)
Deer are susceptible to this disease and Karstad *et al.* (1956) reported a survey of natural cases. Subsequently, this virus produced cases experimentally in white-tailed deer. It appears that at least some species of deer are highly susceptible but usually only a mild disease results with rapid recovery. An insect vector may well be involved and infection may even be associated with entry of the virus at sites damaged by screw worms. Laboratory examinations are essential for differential diagnosis particularly from F.M.D. It is probable that deer constitute the main natural source of virus.

Rabies
Although deer of various species are liable to develop clinical rabies if they come into contact with the virus, they do not constitute a serious problem in nature. Outbreaks have been encountered in park deer and the outbreak in Richmond Park in the last century is well documented; but on the whole the cases in deer are accidents and incidental to the usual perpetuation of the infection in nature. The disease is associated with excitement, antagonism, unco-ordination, and eventual paralysis; on the whole cases are very rare although at at least seven different cervine species have been involved so far.

Pseudorabies (Aujesky's disease)
This is also a very rare disease in deer although of considerable importance to the individual animal. It has been reported in roe from Yugoslavia by Mikolitsch (1954), and from red deer in Germany by Bouvier and others (1958). The clinical signs consist of marked itching and hyperaesthesia.

Bacterial Diseases

So far as deer are concerned, few diseases caused by bacteria appear to be of much significance. Individual deer may develop a variety of superficial pyogenic conditions, involving the skin and occasionally the deeper tissues. Even the joints can be affected in rare instances, but most of these infections are associated with previous external damage, e.g. skin penetration from thorns and other sharp objects along the deer tracks in thick cover, and sometimes from injury by other deer's antlers. The bacteria merely invade the damaged tissue and give rise to abscesses. The corynebacteria are frequently responsible for this and staphylococci and streptococci are also sometimes involved. These are individual cases and do not constitute a herd problem. There are, however, a few bacterial diseases which are of considerable importance to deer.

Brucellosis
Although of little significance in most species of deer, brucellosis is of importance in caribou and reindeer *Rangifer* sp. The causal organism (*B. rangiferi*) is closely related to *B. suis* and can cause considerable clinical trouble, not only in the caribou and reindeer herds, but also in their attendants (Neiland *et al.*, 1968). Few reliable records exist in other species and in an extensive study of the situation in the United Kingdom at a time when there was plenty of infection in the cattle population, there was very little evidence of antibody in the blood of deer of various species and the organism has never been recovered from their foetuses or foetal membranes (McDiarmid & Matthews, 1974). This is surprising in view of the fact that the erythritol content of the deer's uterus, when compared to that of the cow, is sufficient to support the growth of this organism in that particular location (Roberts *et al.*, 1976). On the continent of Europe several isolated cases have been recorded, particularly in roe, e.g. by Schiel (1936) and Preum (1936) in Germany. Cases have also been described in Switzerland by Burgisser (1954), but these are rare.

Tuberculosis
Very few cases of the bovine or human types of infection have ever been recorded in free-living wild deer. Some have occurred in zoological and other parks, usually associated with a clear cut source of infection. Avian strains of various types can, however, often be isolated from apparently healthy deer and on occasions can cause clinical disease, particularly in red deer (McDiarmid, 1975).

A survey of the ileocaecal lymph nodes has revealed a high carriage rate in some species, e.g. roe deer in the United Kingdom (26 per cent) and it is interesting to note that the species producing the majority of clinical cases has only a 5 per cent carriage rate. Confusion could have existed in the past when it was said that deer could develop paratuberculosis, a condition associated with another member of the mycobacterial group. It is more likely that these cases were due to aberrant forms of the avian bacillus, as no cases of paratuberculosis have been found in deer in recent years.

Leptospirosis

Cases of this disease are extremely rare in deer in the United Kingdom (Twigg *et al.*, 1973) but in some other countries it is considered to be important. Much of the investigational work has been done in the last 20 years, particularly in the U.S.A. where the interest of the research workers has centred mainly on the white-tailed deer. In Illinois, 10 per cent carried antibody for *L. pomona* (Ferris *et al.*, 1961) and 16 per cent were positive serologically to the same organism in Minnesota (Wedman and Driver, 1957). The infection cannot be detected clinically in unbred deer but can cause abortion in pregnant animals. Several isolations of *L. pomona* have now been made in the U.S.A. and Canada and other serotypes have occasionally been recovered. Much more evidence is required concerning the precise significance of letospirosis in deer, but in the meantime its possible importance must not be under-estimated in various parts of the world.

Salmonellosis and clostridial infections

In an extensive search for Salmonellosis in deer in the U.K., McDiarmid (1975) isolated one strain of *S. dublin* from a fallow deer in the New Forest. Deer appear to be extremely resistant to infection with Salmonellae and there are very few records elsewhere in the world. Clostridial infections are also virtually non-existent and this is surprising when one considers the opportunities deer have for contracting such diseases from domestic farm stock. Anthrax is the exception. In recent years it seems to have assumed greater importance and it has been pointed out that in the Etosha National Park in South Africa 54 per cent of all the mortality in wildlife was caused by this disease. Most wild animals appear to have a considerable degree of resistance, deer being no exception, but this can readily be broken down by stresses of various kinds, such as overcrowding and degenerated habitats. In the past however, it is believed anthrax outbreaks killed vast numbers of deer in Europe, e.g. in 1874 in Prussia 2000 red deer and fallow deer are considered to have died from this disease (Wetzel and Rieck, 1966); these authors state that the disease still occurs in red, fallow, roe deer and elk in Europe, Anthrax has also been reported in deer in several States in the U.S.A.

The clinical signs of the disease vary considerably; it may cause death in two or three days or a more chronic infection ensues, but the main signs are similar to those in cattle, namely sudden death in the peracute type, with a frothy bloody discharge from the nostrils, and dark tarry-looking blood from the natural orifices in the less acute cases. It must be stressed, however, the disease can readily be confused with other conditions and it is essential that microscopic and bacteriological methods are employed for diagnosis.

Protozoal Diseases

Various protozoal diseases are known to exist in deer of various species but their roles in the production of disease are still merely speculative in most instances. This applies particularly to diseases such as sarcosporidiosis which occurs in mule deer and elk and toxoplasmosis which has been described in numerous species. It has been suggested that the animals have to be stressed to provoke any clinical response to these agents. On the other hand, some diseases of protozoal origin are of significance more for their possible impact on farm livestock.

Piroplasmosis

The causal agent of red water fever is *Babesia bigemina*, the infection is tick-transmitted, and the symptoms are basically, fever, anaemia and haemoglobinuria. White-tailed deer, particularly in the Panama region, and reindeer in the tundra of the far north, are commonly affected. Deer might well be a reservoir of this infection in the enzootic areas. It is, however, probable that these blood parasites could be host specific. Recently, in the U.K., it has been shown that roe deer and red deer carry Babesia. Transmission experiments in splenectomised bovine calves have so far failed, although the infection has been transmitted to susceptible red deer calves by experimental inoculation.

Anaplasmosis

This infection is now considered to be spread widely throughout the temperate zones as well as in the warmer areas. It can be transmitted by a wide range of insects from ticks to stable flies and mosquitoes. The affected animals can show pronounced anaemia without haemogloburinia. In contrast to red water fever, infection has been transmitted from deer to cattle by experimental inoculation. Although deer in enzootic areas probably act as silent reservoirs of this infection and show no clinical signs, the possibility exists that other species of deer brought into such areas might become clinically affected.

Rickettsial Infections

Q fever antibody has been demonstrated in white-tailed deer in the U.S.A. but no significant clinical disease has been reported. Likewise, tick borne fever (T.B.F.) originally thought to be a rickettsial infection and now classified in the genus *Cytoecetes*, is common in all the main species of deer in the tick-infested areas in the U.K. without apparent clinical disease. The infection can readily be transmitted to cattle and sheep by experimental inoculation and it can cause abortion in these animals. It also plays an important part in the establishment of other disease such as Louping ill (meningoencephalomeningitis) and staphylococcal infection in lambs; introduced susceptible deer from a non-tick area might well exhibit similar symptoms on their first meeting with the T.B.F. agent.

Neoplastic Disease

Several varieties of tumours have been found in a wide range of deer species. They are of little significance so far as the herd is concerned, but they are of interest from the medical/veterinary angle. Lymphosarcoma is probably the most common; frequently it can be fatal in fallow and roe deer. Red deer in Scotland are affected with skin tumours of a fibrous nature, very similar to those described in the U.S.A. They appear to be species-specific and cattle cannot be infected by experimental inoculation.

Ectoparasites

On the whole, these are of little significance so far as mortality is concerned, except where the parasites are acting as vectors for an insect-borne disease. In the United Kingdom the warble fly (*Hypoderma diana*) can play havoc with the skins of red deer, thereby greatly reducing their market value. Mortality can occur where the wounds from the emerging warble larvae are parasitised by other insects. Likewise the nasal or bot fly (*Cephenomyia auribaris*) probably occurs throughout Britain but again it is the red deer in the North of Scotland which are mainly affected. Several species of *Cephenomyia* are involved with the black-tailed deer, mule deer and white-tailed deer in the U.S.A. and Canada; sometimes elk and moose are also affected. Deaths have been attributed to heavy infestations of these parasites. In the warm summer months the head fly (*Hydrotaea irritans*) can cause great distress and could be associated with the deer's diminished food intake at that time of year. Lice seem to be of little significance and the deer keds, apart from causing debility if they are present in large numbers, are not important parasites. The ticks, however, are of importance, not so much for their own blood-sucking activities but mainly because of the infections they transmit such as tick-borne fever, louping ill and red water fever. These are all of considerable importance to farm livestock but the local deer do not appear to suffer any serious disease from any of them. It is interesting to note that in the U.S.A., prior to the screw worm fly eradication programme initiated in 1958/9 by the U.S. Department of Agriculture, 80 per cent of the deer fawns in certain areas in Texas were killed by these parasites. Deer herds in Florida have increased by 60 per cent since this parasite was controlled by releasing adult screw worm flies rendered sterile by exposure to radioactive cobalt in the pupal stage. The object of this exercise was to try to reduce the infection of wounds of farm stock with this parasite but, indirectly, deer and other wildlife benefitted greatly from this technique. There are many recorded instances where deer have become infected with these parasites when sharing their habitat with farm animals. Rare cases have occurred where the developing antlers of male deer, in the velvet stage, have been parasitised by flies and the larvae from their eggs have penetrated through the skull, causing death. Attempts at introducing deer to a new area have been thwarted by these parasites, which the deer collected from decaying seaweed. In one particular instance no male deer survived and the attempt at translocation had to be abandoned.

Endoparasites

With rare exceptions, much has yet to be discovered concerning helminths in deer. Many, especially those in the intestinal tract, are common to various species of deer and domestic animals. They are mostly *Trichostrongylus* spp. in the abomasum particularly *T. axei*; generally the worm burden is low in the small intestine. Under natural conditions, the helminths in the intestinal tract are of little importance with regard to disease but this situation can alter dramatically under bad conditions of management, e.g. too many animals in a confined space, or a badly run park. Two important helminths of deer, particularly in the U.K., are *Fasciola hepatica*, the common liver-fluke, and a *Dictyocaulus* sp. of lungworm. Clinical disease is rarely encountered, unless management is bad, but roe deer appear particularly susceptible to both parasites, particularly the latter which is responsible for causing considerable mortality, often as much as 16 per cent of the yearlings. Lungworm is undoubtedly the main factor concerned with the difficulty of keeping roe deer in small enclosures and this could well apply to more exotic species as well. Several species of deer appear resistant to these two infections. This is most noticeable in areas where sheep are present as well as red deer. Often there is high mortality in the sheep and yet the deer show low egg counts in their faeces and only slight fibriotic scarring in their livers (McDiarmid, 1975). Work in Canada has also confirmed that white-tailed deer are extremely resistant to experimental infection with *Fasciola hepatica* (Presidente *et al.*, 1975). Liver fluke disease is virtually unknown in sika deer living under natural conditions in the United Kingdom. Roe deer will, however, often die from liver fluke, particularly in areas such as the west of Scotland, where it is the main controlling factor on the population. The disease in roe closely resembles the condition in sheep. Severe outbreaks of liver fluke disease have occurred in various species of park deer, where the management has been at fault. Often the situation can be remedied by fencing off the snail habitat, e.g. marshy ground. Another parasitic condition, prevalent in North American deer, affects the central nervous system. This neurological disease is often known as 'moose sickness'. It is basically a cerebrospinal nematodiasis caused by *Parelaphostrongylus tenuis*, which invades the cranial subdural space and cranial venous sinuses. The parasite's main host appear to be the white-tailed deer but moose and wapiti can be severely affected. The presence of the disease in moose seems to be associated with the spread of the white-tailed deer. Environmental changes in the last twenty years have in many instances brought this species into close contact with other cervids such as the moose, the mule deer and woodland caribou to the north of its established range. It is interesting to note that severe disease has been caused in fallow deer and this must serve as a warning that more exotic deer could also be highly susceptible if brought into contact with it. Another serious parasitic disease, particularly of elk, which causes blindness, deformed ears and antler damage, as well as affecting the central nervous system, is caused by the filarial worm *Elaeophora schneideri*, often called the arterial or blood worm. It is widespread throughout the west and south-west U.S.A.

General Factors Concerning Disease and Deer

It is usually appreciated that the fewer animals in the herd the less risk of them contracting disease, but the important point, so far as deer are concerned, is that many diseases are transmitted from other species, including farm livestock such as cattle and sheep. The mixing of a group of deer with farmstock directly, or even indirectly, in adjacent paddocks, is liable to produce a situation where certain infections could easily pass to the deer. We have good evidence that this has already happened with viral diseases, such as Foot and Mouth Disease, Malignant Catarrh and Rinderpest, and in some instances direct contact was not required, the virus being transmitted by imported feeding stuffs. Likewise, the burden of endoparasites which deer might have to bear, can readily be augmented by mixed grazing with cattle and/or sheep, particularly the latter; often this extra load of internal parasites is sufficient in conjunction with the deer's own specific parasites to tip the balance between host and parasites and precipitate clinical disease. It seems probable on the present evidence, which admittedly is scanty, that the most important diseases to guard against are the viral infections, as some of these often produce a very high level of mortality and little can be done to save the animals.

The endoparasites generally produce a much slower type of clinical condition and are, in many instances, amenable to treatment with appropriate vermicides. Provided the range of habitat is large enough and overstocking is not practised, it is seldom such drastic action is needed.

Disease Investigations in Deer Field Work

Under primitive conditions in the field it is always very difficult or even impossible, to determine the precise cause of death of any animal. It is difficult enough even in the Highlands of Scotland far more in the wilderness of South America or the forests or mountains of the Far East. Firstly, the animals have often been dead for some time prior to discovery and this often precludes any reasonable microscopic examination being done. Sometimes, however, the internal organs are still worth examining and this applies particularly to the endoparasites in the alimentary tract. Ectoparasites may also provide some clues, e.g. heavy tick infestation. The main point is to try to know the normal appearance of all the tissues and thus be able to identify any deviations, e.g. the lungs looking like liver tissue. Any nodules, particularly in the thorax or abdominal cavities, are always worth further investigation although probably only by fixation of the tissues and subsequent sectioning. Tuberculosis can often be detected in this way. Careful notes should be made of any evidence of haemorrhages in the different organs.

If the tissues are fresh and facilities for laboratory examination are not too far distant, then attempts at cultivating a possible causal agent may be made from the viscera or the heart blood. Probably the most useful material of all is a blood sample taken from the animal if still alive, even the clotted blood from the heart of a deer which has recently died can be useful. When the serum is recovered from such a sample, much can sometimes be discovered by various antibody tests for viruses and bacterial infections. Dried films, prepared from the animal's blood and fixed if possible, are sometimes useful so far as the blood-borne protozoa are concerned. Faecal pellets may reveal the presence of liver fluke eggs or those of other endoparasites. Urine, if fresh, may show the presence of leptospires if facilities for such examinations are close at hand.

Probably the best policy for any field biologist who wishes to study the health status of any deer species is to contact the local veterinary services well in advance to find out the prevalence of certain diseases in the domesticated stock, if any, in the study area, and discuss the ways and means of handling samples from the deer for examination. A code of practice might then be established and whatever laboratory facilities are present in the area might be put at the investigator's disposal. Very few diseases can be diagnosed, with certainty, by non-qualified personnel – often it is difficult enough for trained veterinary surgeons. Moreover, laboratory facilities are nearly always essential for differential diagnosis, particularly in many of the more important viral diseases, and to try to attempt to identify the cause of illness or death of a deer without them is virtually impossible.

Deer Management and Disease

From the foregoing, it will be appreciated that there are many close links between Management and disease. Little can be done under natural conditions where animals are free-living in an uncontrolled environment, but even there, attempts can sometimes be made to improve the situation by encouraging the type of browse or herbage favoured by the deer and attempting to create an undisturbed habitat by controlling poaching activities. Tourism can often be as great a hazard as poaching from the disturbance point of view. When the deer are confined in an enclosed fenced park, much more can be done. Firstly, an adequate food supply must be maintained suitable for the species. The water supply must be reliable and free from contamination. If there is a marshy piece of ground where snails, the intermediate hosts for liver fluke, are present, this should be fenced off, drained or treated with a snail-killing agent. The most important point of all is to try to avoid a situation where the deer are sharing the grazing with farm livestock, particularly sheep. If it is practicable, some form of rotational grazing is a great advantage. Sometimes more than one species of deer can be accommodated in the same park, provided their health history is available before introduction to the park. Adequate cover must always be available for parturition and shelter for the subsequent fawns; suitable fraying stocks for the males to clean their antlers on are always desirable. The actual stocking rate is very important and the correct sex and age ratios for the species must be assessed very carefully so as to maintain the normal behaviour pattern within the herd. Any sick animals must be isolated at once and if veterinary help is at hand an attempt must be made to reach an accurate diagnosis and institute the correct treatment at a very early stage. At all times, stress must be avoided and if it is necessary to handle the deer suitable dart weapons and drugs should be available. These must not, however, be used indiscriminately as there is always a risk of individual idiosyncrasy and fatalities can result with certain species according to the drugs.

References

Bouvier, G., Burgisser, H. & Sneider, P. (1958) Les maladies des Ruminants Sauvages de la Suisse, Institut Galli-Valerio, Lausanne.

Burgisser, H. (1954) Premier cas de Brucellose du chevreuil signalé en Suisse. *Rev. Path. gén comp.* **54**: 124–126.

Cheatum, E.L. & Severinghaus, C.W. (1950). Variations in the fertility of Whitetailed deer. *Trans. N. Amer. Wildl. Conf.* **15**: 170–190.

Curasson, G. (1932). *La peste Bovine*. Vigot Frères, Paris.

Ferris, D.H., Hanson, L.E., Rhoades, H.E. & Aberts, J.O. (1961). Bacteriologic and Serologic investigations of Brucellosis and

Leptospirosis in Illionois Deer. *J. Am. Vet. Med. Assoc.* **139**: 892–896.

Gibbs, E.P.J., Herniman, K.A.J., Lawman, M.J.P. & Sellers, R.F. (1975). Foot and Mouth Disease in British Deer: transmission of virus to cattle, sheep and deer. *Vet. Rec.*, June 28th, 558–563.

Gibbs, E.P.J., & Lawman, M.J.P. (1977). Infection of British Deer and farm animals with Epizootic Haemorrhagic disease of deer virus. *J. Comp. Path.* **87**: 335–352.

Gupta, K.C.S. & Verma, N.S. (1949). Rinderpest in Wild Ruminants. *Indian J. Vet. Sci.* **19**: 219.

Hayes, F.H., Greer, W.E. & Shotts, E.B. (1957). Progress Report from the South

Eastern Co-operative Deer Disease Study. *Trans. N. Amer. Wildl. Conf.* 21: 133–136.

Hamby, F.M., Dardiri, A.H., Ferris, D.H. & Breese, S.S. (1975). Experimental Infection of Whitetailed Deer with Rinderpest Virus. *J. Wildl. Dis.* 11: 508–515.

Hoff, G.L., Trainer, D.O. & Jochim, M.M. (1974). Bluetongue Virus and White-tailed Deer in an Enzootic Area of Texas. *J. Wildl. Dis.* 10: 158–163.

Huck, R.A., Shand, A., Allsop, P.S. & Paterson, A.B. (1961). Malignant Catarrh of Deer. *Vet. Rec.* 73: 457–465.

Jones, R.H., Roughton, R.D., Foster, N.M. & Bando, B.M. (1977). *Culicoides* The Vector of Epizootic Haemorrhagic Disease in White-tailed Deer in Kentucky in 1971. *J. Wildl. Dis.* 13: 2–8.

Karstad, L.H. Adams, R.P., Hanson, R.P. & Ferris, D.H. (1956). Evidence for the role of Wildlife in epizootics of Vesicular Stomatitis. *J. Amer. Vet. Med. Assoc.* 129: 95–96.

McDiarmid, A. & Matthews, P.R.J. (1974). Brucellosis in Wildlife. *Vet. Rec.*, June 15th, 559.

McDiarmid, A. (1974). Mortality in Deer. *Mammal Review* 4: 75–78.

McDiarmid, A. (1975). Some disorders of wild deer in the United Kingdom. *Vet. Rec.*, July 5th, 6–9.

Murray, J.O. & Trainer, D.O. (1970). Bluetongue Virus in North American Elk. *J. Wildl. Dis.* 6: 144–148.

Neiland, K.A., King, J.A., Huntley, B.E. & Skoog, R.O. (1968). The Diseases and Parasites of Alaskan Wildlife Populations. *Bull. Wildl. Dis. Assoc.* 4: 27–36.

Nikolitsch, M. (1954). Die Aujeszkysche Krankheit beim Reh. *Wien. Tierartztl. Monatsch* 41: 603.

Presidente, P.J.A., McCraw, B.M. & Lumsden, J.H. (1974). Pathologic features of experimentally induced *Fasciola hepatica* infection in white-tailed deer. *Wildl. Dis.* 63.

Preun, B. (1938). Arthritis und Tendovaginitis durch Brec. abortus Bang bei einem Rehbock. *Dtsch. tierärztl. Wschr.* 46: 804.

Richards, S.H., Schipper, I.A., Eveleth, D.F. & Shumard, R.I. (1956). Mucosal Disease of Deer. *Vet. Med.* 51: 358–362.

Roberts, G.P., McDiarmid, A. & Gleed, P. (1976). The presence of erythritol in the fetal fluids of fallow deer (*Dama dama*). *Res. vet. Sci.* 20: 254–256.

Sanford, S.E., Little, P.B. & Rapley, W.A. (1977). The Gross and Histopathologic Lesions of Malignant Catarrhal Fever in three captive Sika deer (*Cervus nippon*) in Southern Ontario. *J. Wildl. Dis.* 13: 29–32.

Schiel, O. (1936). Abortus-Bang-Bakteriennachweis im Hoden eines Rehbockes. *Z. Fleisch-u Milchhyg.* 47: 114.

Scott, G.R. (1976). Wildlife Rinderpest. In L.A. Page (ed.) *Wildlife Diseases*. Plenum Press, New York, Pp. 245–255.

Shope, R.E., MacNamara, L.G. & Mangold, R. (1955). Report on the Deer Mortality, epizootic haemorrhagic disease of deer. *New Jersey Outdoors* 6(5): 16–21.

Shope, R.E., MacNamara, L.G. & Mangold, R. (1960). A virus induced epizootic haemorrhagic disease of the Virginia white-tailed deer (*Odocoileus virginianus*). *J. Exptl. Med.* 111: 155–170.

Thomas, F.C. & Prestwood, A.K. (1976). Plaque Neutralisation Test Reactors to Bluetongue and EHD Viruses in the South Eastern U.S.A. In L.A. Page (ed.) *Wildlife Diseases*. Plenum Press, New York. Pp. 401–411.

Twigg, G.I., Hughes, D.M. & McDiarmid, A. (1973). The low incidence of leptospirosis in British deer. *Vet. Rec.*, July 28th, 98–100.

Wedman, E.E. & Driver, F.C. (1957). Leptospirosis and Brucellosis titres in Deer Blood. *J. Amer. Vet. Med. Assoc.* 130: 513–514.

Wetzel, R. & Rieck, W. (1966). *Les maladies du Gibier*. Librairie Maloine, Paris.

Much of this information has already appeared in the Proceedings of the Working Meeting of the I.U.C.N. Survival Service Commission Deer Specialist Group at Longview, Washington State, U.S.A. in 1977, as published by I.U.C.N., Morges, Switzerland in 1978.

Reference Section

1 DEER AND THE LAW

This section attempts to answer some questions commonly asked about the law as it affects deer. While every effort has been made to ensure accuracy, no responsibility is taken and anyone concerned with deer should obtain copies of the various Acts, Orders and Regulations and refer to them in all cases of doubt. The legal position in Scotland is particularly complex and in most cases different from that applying in England and Wales.

Legislation Relating to Deer

England and Wales	Scotland
Game Licences Act 1860	Deer (Scotland) Act 1959
Deer Act 1991	S.I. 1966 No. 56 (S.4) The Deer (Close Seasons) (Scotland) Order 1966
	Deer (Amendment) (Scotland) Act 1967
	Sale of Venison (Scotland) Act 1968
	S.I. 1969 No. 794 (S.63) The Sale of Venison (Forms etc.) (Scotland) Regulations 1969
	Deer (Amendment) (Scotland) Act 1982

Statutory Close Seasons for Deer (all dates inclusive)

Species	Sex	England and Wales	
Red	stags	1 May — 31 July	
	hinds	1 Mar — 31 Oct	
Fallow	buck	1 May — 31 July	
	doe	1 Mar — 31 Oct	'63 Act
Sika	stags	1 May — 31 July	Sched. 1
	hinds	1 Mar — 31 Oct	
Roe	buck	1 Nov — 31 Mar	'77 Act
	doe	1 Mar — 31 Oct	

		Scotland	
Red	stags	21 Oct — 30 June	
	hinds	16 Feb — 20 Oct	
Fallow	buck	1 May — 31 July	
	doe	16 Feb — 20 Oct	'59 Act
Sika	stags	1 May — 31 July	S.I. 1966/56
	hinds	16 Feb — 20 Oct	
Roe	buck	21 Oct — 30 Apr	
	doe	1 Mar — 20 Oct	

Note: As a generalisation, the prevention of suffering by injured or diseased deer provides an exception to the law affecting close seasons, night shooting and prohibited weapons etc. Reference should be made to the appropriate Act or Order.

England and Wales

Close Season Shooting

It is an offence for any person to take or wilfully kill any deer
during the close season unless, if charged, he can prove to the   '63 Act S.1.
satisfaction of the court that he was an authorised person and   '81 Act
that –   Sched. 7

a   he had reasonable grounds for believing that deer of the
same species were causing or had caused damage to crops,
growing timber, etc. on the land on which the action was taken;

b   further such damage was likely and would have been
serious, and

c   his action was necessary to prevent such damage.

An 'authorised person' means:

1   the occupier of the land on which the action is taken;

2   a member of the occupier's household normally resident on
the occupier's land acting with his written permission;

3   a person in the ordinary service of the occupier on the
occupier's land acting with his written permission or

4   a person having the right to take or kill deer on the land on
which the action is taken or a person acting with the written
permission of a person having that right.

Deer may be taken during the close season only by means of
shooting and only on cultivated land, pasture or enclosed
woodland.
    Other exceptions are allowed for certain purposes under   '63 Act
licence issued by the Nature Conservancy Council, or to   Ss. 10, 11
comply with a requirement of M.A.F.F. under S.98 of the
Agriculture Act 1947.

Scotland

Close Season Shooting

It is an offence to take, wilfully kill or injure any red, fallow, sika or roe deer in the close season laid down according to species and sex.
Exceptions as follows:–

'59 Act
S.21
S.I. 1966/56
'82 Act S.6

Authorised	Reason	Species	
Red Deer Commission Staff (R.D.C.)	Serious damage to agricultural land or woodland or gardens or injury to farm animals including serious overgrazing of pasture	Any deer	'82 Act Ss.3,4
Competent person authorised by R.D.C.	As above	Red, sika, hybrids	'82 Act S.3
Owner in person, with written authority from occupier	Belief that serious damage would be caused to crops, pasture, trees or foodstuffs if deer are not killed. Applies only to arable land, garden grounds, permanent grass *except* moorland and unenclosed land, and enclosed woodland.	Any deer	'82 Act S.13
and	Period specified by occupier or R.D.C.		
Owner's servants, authorised in writing by occupier			
and			
Occupier in person			
and			
Servants of occupier authorised by him in writing			
and			
Competent person approved by R.D.C. and authorised in writing by occupier			
Deer Farmers and their servants	Provided deer are marked and kept in a deer-proof enclosure		'82 Act S.7

England and Wales

Night Shooting

It is an offence to take, kill or injure deer at night (1 hour after sunset to 1 hour before sunrise).

'63 Act
S.1

'81 Act
Sched.7

Scotland

Night Shooting

It is an offence to take or wilfully kill or injure deer at night (1 hour after sunset to 1 hour before sunrise)
Exceptions as follows:

'59 Act
S.23

Authorised	Reason	Species	
R.D.C. Staff	As Close Season Shooting (above)	Any deer	'82 Act Ss.3,4
Occupier in person	Threat of serious damage to crops, pasture, trees or foodstuffs if deer are not killed.	Red, sika, hybrids	'82 Act S.13
	Only if		
Competent person authorised by occupier and R.D.C. in writing	(a) shooting is necessary to prevent serious damage to crops etc; and (b) no other method of control which might reasonably be adopted in the circumstances would be adequate; and (c) that the person concerned is a fit and competent person to receive such authorisation. The period to be specified by R.D.C.	Any deer	'82 Act S.13

Note: A Code of Practice for night shooting has been published by R.D.C. and anyone authorised to shoot at night must adhere to it.

'82 Act

England and Wales

Weapons

The following are banned for killing, injuring or taking deer:

a   Any rifle of less than .240″ calibre or ammunition giving a muzzle energy less than 1700ft/lb;

'63 Act
Sched.2

b   any airgun, air rifle or air pistol;

c   any rifle bullet other than a soft- or hollow-nosed bullet;

d   any arrow, spear or similar missile;

'63 Act
S.3

e   any missile, discharged from a firearm or otherwise, carrying or containing any poison, stupefying drug or muscle-relaxing agent;

f   any shotgun.

'81 Act
Sched.7

Exception: A shotgun may be used to kill deer to control damage, but only:

'81 Act
Sched.7

a   by an Authorised Person, as defined under Close Season Shooting, above; and

b   under the same circumstances as set out in **a**, **b** and **c** in that section; and

c   if the shotgun is 12 bore (or larger) with cartridges loaded with AAA shot or rifled slug.

Prohibited Methods of Taking and Killing Deer

traps, snares, nets, poisoned or stupefying bait.

'63 Act
S.3

Note: The exception with regard to injured or diseased deer only applies to traps and nets.

Scotland

Weapons

It is an offence to take or wilfully kill or injure deer otherwise than by shooting. This excludes snares, bows and arrows and the like.	'59 Act S.23
Note: Authorised persons may take deer alive in Scotland, provided the deer are not caused unnecessary suffering.	'59 Act S.23

England and Wales

Vehicles

Shooting deer from or driving deer with a vehicle is an offence. '63 Act
'Vehicle' includes aircraft or helicopter.   S.3

Exception: When done by or with the written authority of
the occupier of enclosed land where deer are usually kept, in
relation to that land.

Game Licences

A game licence is needed to kill or take deer.   1860 Act
                                                          S.4

Exceptions: Taking or killing deer on any enclosed land by   1860 Act
the owner or occupier, or with his permission.   S.5

Scotland

Vehicles

It is an offence to use a vehicle for driving deer on unenclosed land with the intention of taking killing, or injuring them. ('Vehicle' includes aircraft, helicopter or any 'conveyance' except a public service vehicle.)	'82 Act S.9
It is an offence to shoot or discharge any missile at deer from an aircraft.	'82 Act S.8
It is an offence to transport live deer by air other than in the interior of the aircraft. Aircraft includes helicopter.	
Exception: Deer may be transported by air other than inside the aircraft by, or under the supervision of, a veterinary surgeon or practitioner.	

Game Licences

A game licence is needed to kill or take deer.	1860 Act S.4
Exceptions: Taking or killing deer on any enclosed land by the owner or occupier, or with his permission.	1860 Act S.5
Any person authorised or required by R.D.C. to kill deer under Part 1 of the Deer (Scotland) Act.	'59 Act S.14

England and Wales

Sale of Venison

Venison may only be sold to a licensed game dealer.	'80 Act S.2

Venison may not be purchased by a licensed game dealer during the prohibited period, except from another licensed game or venison dealer. The 'prohibited period' for any species and description of deer for which a close season is prescribed means the period beginning with the expiration of the tenth day, and ending with the expiration of the last day, of that season.	'80 Act S.2

Buying, selling or receiving venison taken illicitly is an offence.	'80 Act S.2

Licensed game dealer must keep records which may be inspected by an authorised officer or constable, who may also inspect any venison in dealer's possession.	'80 Act S.3

'Sale' and 'purchase' include barter and exchange.

'Venison' includes any edible part of a deer, including imported, but not canned or cooked venison.	'80 Act S.8

Scotland

Sale of Venison

Venison may only be sold to or purchased from a licensed
venison dealer.

'82 Act
S.11

Licensed venison dealer must keep records which may be
inspected by persons authorised by Secretary of State or
R.D.C. or any constable who may also inspect any venison in
dealer's possession.

Buying, selling or receiving venison taken illicitly is an offence.

'Sale' and 'purchase' includes barter and exchange.

'Venison' includes any edible part of a deer.

England and Wales

Poaching and Other Offences

Entry on any land in search or pursuit of deer without lawful authority.

'80 Act
S.1

Intentionally taking, killing or injuring any deer without lawful authority.

Removing the carcase of any deer without lawful authority.

Attempts to commit offences are equally offences.

'63 Act
S.4

Note: Penalties are calculated as if each deer were a separate offence.

'80 Act
S.2

Scotland

Poaching and Other Offences

Taking, wilfully killing or injuring deer on any land without legal right.	'59 Act S.22
Offences committed by two or more persons together (aggravated offence).	'59 Act S.24
Removing the carcase of any deer without legal authority.	'82 Act S.6
Unlawful possession of deer.	'59 Act S.25
Unlawful possession of firearms or ammunition used to commit an offence.	'59 Act S.25
Attempt to commit offences are equally offences.	'59 Act S.26

Note: Penalties are calculated as if each deer were a separate offence.

England and Wales

Powers

A constable or *an authorised person* may ask anyone he suspects of committing an offence:

'80 Act
S.1

1   to give his full name and address; and

2   to quit the land forthwith.

A constable, on reasonable suspicion of an offence, may without warrant:

'80 Act
S.4
and Sched. 2

a   stop and search the suspect;

b   search or examine any vehicle, animal, weapon or other thing which the suspect may be using;

c   arrest the suspect if he fails to give a satisfactory name and address;

d   seize and detain anything which is evidence of the commission of the offence, and any deer, venison, vehicle, animal, weapon or other thing liable to be forfeited.

A constable may enter land other than a dwelling-house if he suspects with reasonable cause that an offence has been or is being committed.

'80 Act
S.5
and Sched.2

Note: Offenders are now liable to very considerable fines and forfeitures. Shotgun and Firearm Certificates and Game Dealer's Licences may also be cancelled.

Scotland

Powers

In addition to his powers under Common Law, *a Constable*   '59 Act
may seize any deer, firearm, ammunition, vehicle or boat liable   S.27
to be forfeited;

he may, by warrant, enter any premises, vehicle or boat for
evidence of an offence, search any suspect and seize any article
which he believes to be evidence;

he may, by reason of urgency, stop and search a vehicle or boat
without warrant, and exercise similar powers of search or
seizure if he suspects that more than one person is involved in
the commission of an offence;

he may arrest, without warrant, anyone found committing an
offence.   .59 Act
S.28

Offenders are now liable to very considerable fines and
forfeitures. Shotgun and Firearm Certificates and Venison
Dealer's Licences may also be cancelled.

2   DEER DISTRIBUTION MAPS

Reproduced by courtesy of the Institute of Terrestrial Ecology
Biological Records Station, Monks Wood Experimental Station;
Crown Copyright reserved.

As at May 1982

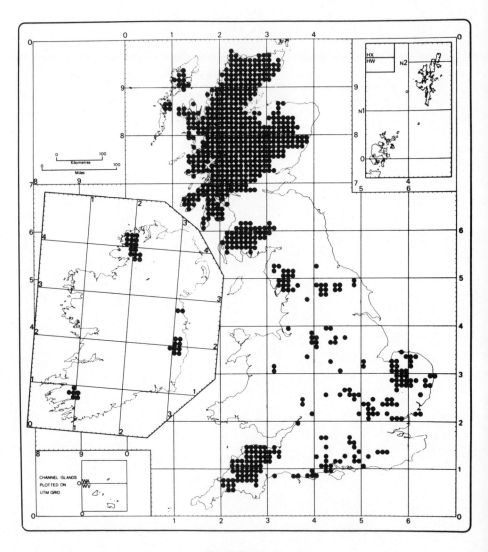

Red Deer

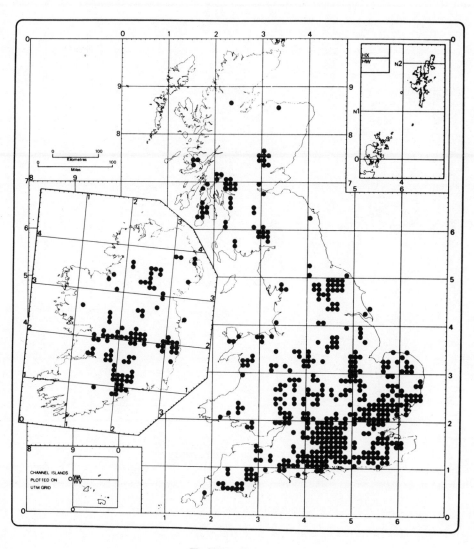

Fallow Deer

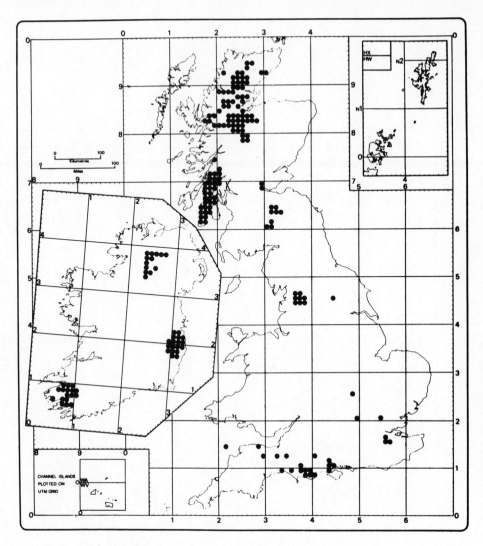

Sika Deer

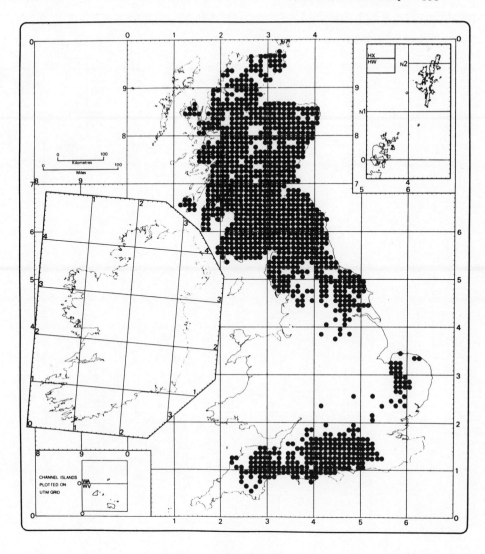

Roe Deer

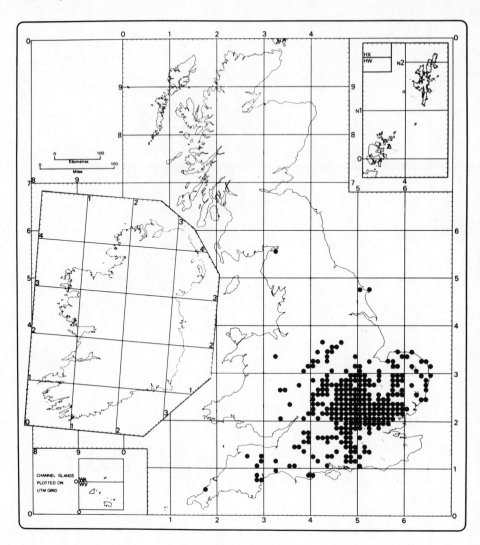

Muntjac

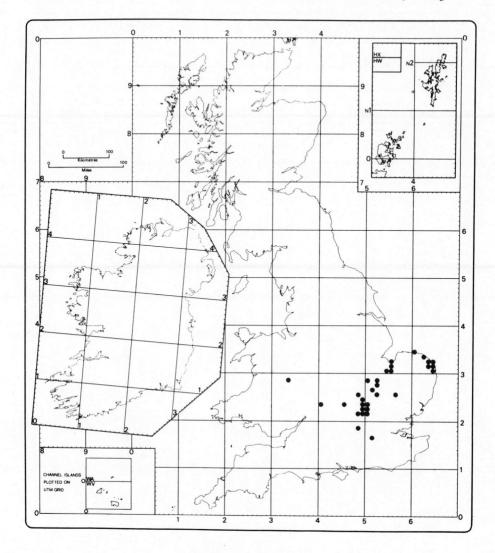

Chinese Water Deer

3   CROPS, SHRUBS AND TREES FOR DEER

Food Plants for Deer

1   *Harvested, stored and hand fed (either main crop or rejects).*

(a) concentrate food (autumn)

		Red*	Roe*
Apples	*Malus sylvestris*	+ +	+ +
Barley	*Hordeum vulgare* (grain)	+ +	+ +
Beet, sugar	*Beta rapa*	+ +	+
Carrots	*Daucus carota*	+ +	+ +
Maize	*Zea mays* (grain)	+ +	+ +
	corn-cob silage	+ +	+
	whole plant silage	+ +	
Mangolds	*Beta vulgaris*	+ +	+
Oats	*Avena sativa* (grain)	+ +	+ +
Potatoes	*Solanum tuberosum*	+ +	+
Rye	*Secale cereale* (grain)	+ +	+ +
Swedes	*Brassica napus*	+ +	+
Wheat	*Triticum aestivum* (grain)	+ +	+ +

(b) maintenance food (winter)
Silage made from whole plants and fruit-husks

		Red	Roe
Apples	*Malus sylvestris*	+ +	+ +
Artichokes, Jerusalem	*Helianthus tuberosus* (herb silage)	+ +	
Beet, fodder	*Beta vulgaris*	+ +	+ +
Beet, sugar	*Beta rapa*	+ +	+ +
Grass-silage		+ +	
Hay		+ +	
Mangolds	*Beta vulgaris*	+ +	+ +

2   *Crops for summer/autumn feed*
(The species in bold type also for winter feed)

		Red	Roe
Artichokes, Jerusalem	*Helianthus tuberosus*	+ +	+ +
Beet, fodder	*Beta vulgaris*	+ +	+ +
Beet, sugar	*Beta rapa*	+ +	+ +
Buckwheat	*Fagopyrum esculentum*	+ +	+ +
Kale	*Brassica oleracea*	+ +	+ +
Linseed	*Linum usitatissimum*	+	+
Lupin, annual sweet	*Lupinus* spp.	+ +	+ +
Maize	*Zea mays*	+ +	+
Mustard	*Sinapis alba*	+ +	
Oats	*Avena sativa*	+ +	+ +
Peas	*Pisum arvense*	+ +	+ +
Radish, fodder	*Raphanus sativus campestris*	+ +	
Rape	*Brassica napus*	+ +	+
Rye	*Secale cereale*	+ +	+ +
Seradella	*Ornithopus sativus*	+ +	
Spurry	*Spergula arvensis*	+ +	
Sunflower	*Helianthus anuus*	+ +	
Swedes	*Brassica napus*	+ +	+
Turnips, stubble (Tyfon)	*Brassica rapa*	+	
Vetches	*Vicia sativa*	+ +	+
Wheat	*Triticum aestivum*	+ +	+ +

3   *Grasses and clovers*

		Red	Roe
Bent grass	*Agrostis* spp.	+	+
Clover alsike	*Trifolium hybridum*	+ +	+
Clover red	*Trifolium pretense*	+ +	+ +
Fescue	*Festuca* spp.	+	+
Foxtail	*Alopecusus* spp.	+	+
Lucerne	*Medicago sativa*	+ +	+ +
Meadow grass – smooth	*Poa pratensis*	+ +	+
Medick black	*Medicago lupulina*	+ +	+
Ryegrass, perennial	*Lolium perenne*	+	
Sainfoin	*Onobrychis sativa*	+ +	+ +
Timothy	*Phleum pratense*	+ +	
Trefoil	*Trifolium resupinatum*	+ +	+
White melilot	*Melilotus albus*	+ +	
Yorkshire fog	*Holcus lanatus*	+	

* Relative benefit to red deer and roe indicated by number of crosses. Fallow and sika have similar tastes to red deer, depending on the location.

Feed Plots

1 Mixtures must be chosen according to the soil and climate, and they must receive suitable fertiliser if they are to flourish and prove attractive to the deer. The following suggestions have been evolved in consultation with Farmacre Seeds Ltd, Tilston, Malpas, Cheshire, from whom seed may be obtained.

Mixture A: fodder root mixture for use on medium to good agricultural land and with reasonable applications of compound fertiliser. The constituents are reasonably winter-hardy and can be expected to last into January.
   Sow May to July.

1.00kg Thousand Headed Kale
1.00kg Maris Kestrel Kale
0.50kg Purple Top Swede
0.50kg Giant Rape
0.50kg Tyfon Stubble Turnip
0.25kg Green Globe Turnip

3.75kg per acre (9.25kg per hectare)

Mixture B: fodder root mixture for upland areas and less fertile conditions. This mixture does however require reasonable soil and will not thrive in very acid conditions.
   Sow July.

3.50kg Giant Rape
0.50kg Green Globe Turnip
6.00kg Danish Italian Ryegrass

9.50kg per acre (23.5kg per hectare)

Mixture C: grass mixture for use in relatively poor soil conditions, as found in hill areas with high rainfall and on woodland rides in sandy soil. This mixture will tolerate acidity but the herbage will be more palatable if lime is applied from time to time.

Sow between April and August.

3.50kg Highland Bent (*Agrostis Tenuis*)
5.50kg Creeping Red Fescue (*Festuca Rubra*)
2.50kg Sheeps Fescue (*Festuca Ovina*)
2.50kg Smooth-stalked Meadow Grass (*Poa Pratensis*)
0.25kg Birds Foot Trefoil (*lotus Corniculatus*)
0.25kg Wild White Clover

14.50kg per acre (36kg per hectare)

4   Herbs

Anemone	*Anemone nemorosa*
Brooklime	*Veronica beccabunga*
Campion red	*Lychnis dioica*
Campion white	*Lychnis alba*
Celandine	*Ranunculus ficaria*
Cinquefoil hoary	*Potentilla argentea*
Dandelion	*Taraxacum officinalis*
Knotweed	*Polygonum aviculare*
Lupin, sweet	*Lupinus luteus*
Meadowsweet	*Filipendula ulmaria*
Redleg	*Polygonum persicaria*
Ribwort	*Plantaga lanceolata*
Rosebay willow herb	*Chamaenerion angustifolium*
Sorrel	*Rumex acetosa*
Strawberry	*Fragaria vesca*
Vetch purple milk	*Astragalus danicus*
Violet	*Viola* spp.
Yarrow	*Achillea millefolium*

5 Trees and shrubs

Alder buckthorn	*Frangula alnus*
Apple	*Malus pumila*
Aspen	*Populus tremula*
Beech	*Fagus sylvatica*
Bog myrtle	*Myrica gale*
Bramble	*Rubus fruticosus*
Broom	*Sarothamnus scoparius*
Cherry, bird	*Prunus padus*
Chestnut, sweet	*Castanea sativa*
Dogwood	*Cornus sanguinea*
Elder	*Sambucus nigra*
Gean	*Prunus avium*
Guelder rose	*Viburnum opulus*
Hawthorn	*Crataegus monogyna*
Hazel	*Corylus avellana*
Holly	*Ilex aquifolium*
Hornbeam	*Carpinus betulus*
Maple, field	*Acer campestre*
Maple, Norway	*Acer platanoides*
Oak	*Quercus* spp.
Pine, lodgepole	*Pinus contorta*
Poplar	*Populus* spp.
Rowan	*Sorbus aucuparia*
Spindle	*Euonymus europaeus*
Wayfaring tree	*Viburnum lantana*
Whitebeam	*Sorbus aria*
Willows	*Salix* spp.

Species which deer are reluctant to eat

Alder	*Alnus* spp.
Birch	*Betula* spp.
Honeysuckle, Japanese	*Lonicera nitida*
Pine, Austrian	*Pinus nigra*
Pine, Corsican	*Pinus maritima*
Juniper	*Juniperus communis*
Shallon	*Gaultheria shallon*
Snowberry	*Symphoricarpos rivularis*
Rhododendron	*Rhododendron*

Note: Juniper forms a valuable resource in mountainous areas. As it is low on the preference list, it is usually left until other food sources have been consumed, and thus protects the deer from starvation.

4 DRAFT FIVE-DAY ROE STALKING LICENCE AND APPLICATION FORM

FIVE-DAY ROE STALKING LICENCE
Conditions and Fees

(exclusive of VAT which will be added at the appropriate rate)

Cost of stalking licence   ..   ..   ..

Entitles the permit holder to stalk, weather and other circumstances permitting, for the 5-day period commencing Monday . . . .

Including Keeper's time and transport and trophy preparation
And including the right to shoot . . . . small bucks (no refund if these are not taken).

In addition the permit holder has the right to shoot . . . . trophy bucks at the following tariff:
Under 300g   ..   ..   ..
310 to 350g   ..   ..   ..
351 to 400g   ..   ..   ..
401 to 450g   ..   ..   ..
451 to 500g   ..   ..   ..
Over 500g   trophy to be scored according to C.I.C. formula
Silver Medal (115 to 129.9 points) . . . . per C.I.C. point
Gold Medal (130 points and above) . . . . per C.I.C. point

Skulls to be boiled and cut to standard short nose, weighed 24 hours after boiling. If long-nosed, deduct 50g, if full skull, less lower jaw, deduct 100g.

Buck wounded and lost, 50% of estimated price or . . . . whichever is the higher.

Unusual malformed heads – price to be agreed.

CONDITIONS

The permit holder will be required to:
a   be accompanied by, and obey the instructions of the stalker
b   provide his own transport to the forest
c   fire a group of sighting shots on arrival to the satisfaction of the stalker
d   produce a valid Firearms Certificate, Game Licence and Third-Party Insurance cover to the value of at least £1,000,000;
e   indemnify the Estate against any loss, injury or damage which may arise from the exercise of the permit.

The carcase remains the property of the Estate but may, when convenient, be purchased by the permit holder unskinned at wholesale rates.

The Estate reserves the right to suspend or withdraw a permit at any time and their decision in any matters arising from the granting of the permit will be final. *Payment for the Licence should be made on acceptance.* In the event of cancellation or curtailment of the period, no refund will be made unless another taker can be found in time.

The application form includes a declaration that the applicant has seen the Conditions and agrees to them.

FIVE-DAY ROE STALKING LICENCES
APPLICATION FORM

NAME _____

ADDRESS _____

_____

PHONE NUMBER Private _____

Business _____

I wish to apply for a roe stalking licence at
_____ (Estate) for five days beginning
_____ (date)

I understand and accept the conditions as set out on the attached schedule, and have retained a copy for reference.

If a licence is granted I undertake to indemnify the Landowner against all claims for loss, injury or damage that may result from the exercise of the licence.

I will be arriving on _____ (date) about
_____ (time) at _____ and will need
accommodation for _____ persons until
_____ (date) in _____ double/single rooms
(with bath).
Accommodation is not included in the price of licence.

Rifle calibre _____ Firearms Certificate No. _____
Issued by _____ Constabulary

Third Party Insurance Cover: _____
Company: _____

Signature of Applicant:

Date: _____

5   WOODLAND DEERSTALKING: SUGGESTED HEADS OF AGREEMENT FOR A BLOCK LET

1   Names of parties. The right of shooting and stalking deer. Area defined. Rent per annum. Landlord/tenant to pay rates. Date of annual payment.

2   Term of agreement. Notice to be given. Breaks for revision of rent. Right to renewal for further term. (In the case of a projected long-term agreement, a preparatory trial period is recommended.)

3   Right to assign or sub-let defined.

4   Trophies the property of the tenant, landlord retains all venison (or not).

5   No more than . . . rifles stalking at any one time. Tenant may invite guests subject to the approval of the landlord, provided that he is himself in the area.

6   Shooting on Sundays permitted/not permitted.

7   Any infringement of the law or any dangerous shooting will involve termination of the agreement without notice or compensation to the tenant.

8   The tenant liable for all loss or damage in relation to the exercise of the agreement, and is responsible for insuring himself, his keeper and guests against injury and accident, and for third party damage or injury.

9   Landlord to assist with the maintenance of clearings etc. when this can be arranged without prejudice to other estate work. The tenant to pay for this at the rate prevailing at the time.

10   The annual shooting plan to be mutually agreed between landlord and tenant. Any dispute to be subject to arbitration by nominated person or official. The tenant should be informed of the coming year's forestry operations when the shooting plan is discussed.

11   The tenant's obligations:

a Report on deer numbers and prepare a shooting plan for the landlord.

b Shoot to the agreed number of deer, both male and female.

c Maintain close liaison with landlord/agent/head forester/keeper, particularly with regard to shooting dates and times.

d Erect and maintain high seats as agreed between owner and tenant.

e Do such clearance work as may be desired by the tenant and which has been agreed by the landlord.

f Provide the landlord with an annual record of all deer shot, with dates and other necessary details.

The landlord's obligations:

a To allow the tenant quiet enjoyment of his right, concurrent with other state activities.

b The landlord and his employees and any other person controlled by him not to shoot any deer except those wounded or diseased and obviously in pain.

The estate retains the right to kill deer in the event of serious damage on condition that the tenant is first informed, and to complete the cull at the tenant's expense if (say 75 per cent) of the agreed number has not been shot by (say two weeks) before the end of the season.

6 STALKER'S JOB SPECIFICATION: HEADS OF AGREEMENT FOR ENGAGING A STALKER

Duties (see below)

To whom responsible/maintenance of time sheets or diary weekly reporting details

Statement of hours and overtime (usually none)

Salary/Clothing allowance/Holidays

Transport/Private use

Housing/Decorations/Garden/Rent, rates/Electricity, telephone/Fuel

Dogs – obligations and restrictions/Allowance

Equipment/Allowance for use of own

Off-estate stalking
a Part of job
b permitted in free time
c not permitted

Define ownership of all deer products (antlers, teeth etc.)

Possible duties

Estimate deer numbers. Prepare shooting plan

Investigate reports of damage

Prepare for and supervise visits of stalking visitors/tenants

Shoot balance of cull/Retrieve and dress all carcases/prepare tenants' trophies

Maintain close liaison with landlord/agent/forester/keeper/farm tenants etc.

Erect and maintain high seats

Do clearance and ride maintenance

Prepare venison for marketing

Other duties (e.g. tree planting, keepering etc.) to be defined

7   DRAFT HEADS OF AGREEMENT FOR GAME DEALER'S TENDER

FORM OF CONTRACT FOR VENISON SALES

1   Contract to run from . . . . (incl.) to . . . . (incl.)

2   The contractor agrees to buy and the seller agrees to sell venison as available for the whole period as paragraph 1 above at an agreed price of . . . . per lb(kg) subject to the following guidelines.

a Carcases will be weighed not less than 3 hours after gralloching and a standard weight reduction be applied of roe 1lb, fallow/sika 4lb, red 8lb, to allow for cooling and drying.

b Damage resulting from one or both shoulder shots...   ...   Nil reduction

c Damage to saddle or 1 haunch...   ...   .   20% reduction

d Damage to saddle +/or 1 or both haunches...   ...   ...   60% reduction

e Resulting net weight to be on label and invoiced.

3   All carcases to be labelled to include
a Area of origin
b Code/Serial number
c Net weight (as 2[e] above)
d Species
e Sex

4   All carcases to be placed in chill/freezer store within 24 hours of death and notification for collection passed to the contractor within the same period. Onus for any deterioration in the carcase due to delay in collection will pass to the contractor.

5   Terms of payment to the mutual agreement of both parties but in any case all venison to be paid for by the end of the month after month of invoice.

6a By-products to be dealt with by mutual agreement of both parties.
b Pluck i.e. heart–lungs–liver & kidneys to be supplied with the carcase at an agreed price per lb(kg) if required by contractor.

7   In the case of default or disagreement by either party the contract can be terminated by giving notice one to the other. Otherwise the contract will be binding for the stated period only and may not be varied other than by mutual consent.

8   The vendor to bear the onus of informing the contractor when venison is ready for collection. The contractor to bear the onus for collecting the venison having passed to him on receipt of the notification.

9   All carcases to be supplied head and feet off. Neck and chest split and aitch bone sawn to allow haunches to open. All internal organs, windpipe, anal canal and back fat removed.

Notes:

1   The definition of a saddle for the purposes of this contract:
The loin and ribs of the carcase from the fifth rib at the front to the major joint at the rear of the loin between the haunches; 3in of rib included in the saddle from the centre of the back bone.

2   Contract price agreed shall be for the whole period of the contract and will only be varied in exceptional circumstances.

(Approved by the National Game Dealers' Association)

8 DEER MANAGEMENT RECORDS

Simple but accurate records are essential.

The instructions and forms which follow were developed by Deer Management Consultants of Middleton Estate, Longparish, Andover, Hants, from whom supplies can be obtained. Bound stalking registers suitable for deer forests are also published.

Separate sets are produced for roe and red deer, the latter being suitable for all large deer species. Used according to the instructions, they make up a unique system for recording all the necessary information for management, accounting and letting.

Notes on Using the Red Deer Management Record Sheets

These come in two parts, comprising:

I The 'HOUSE' Book – This is a Red Deer Game book in which can be entered the details of each stag shot as the season progresses and at the back there is a SUMMARY from which at a glance one season can be compared with another. The row of boxes marked 'C' to 'over 14' under AGES should have the number of deer shot in each age class, e.g. 8 Two-year-olds, 4 Three-year-olds, 2 Twelve-year-olds etc.

AVERAGE AGE is of course the sum of the ages divided by the number of deer shot.

TOTAL WEIGHT is the sum of the weights of all the carcases and is quite interesting when compared to the number of acres from which the venison has come.

AVERAGE WEIGHT will reflect the age from which the bulk of the cull is taken – (c.f. the bulk of the sheep sales come from the lambs).

The next set of boxes will show how many stags have been shot with similar heads, e.g. 4 five pointers, 2 eight pointers etc.

AVERAGE POINTS is the sum of the preceding columns, not counting the malforms, divided by the number of stags that takes in.

Then there is ample room for photographs, sketches and suitable adjectives to describe the weather.

II The Stalker's Folder.

These are the working records and are in five sections.

Firstly, the ordinary forest journal to which we have added a column to show the weight of each carcase that goes out of the larder i.e. 'VAN WEIGHT' should tally with the dealers pay slip – 'DISPOSAL TO' is for e.g. 'House' – 'Northern Game Meat Ltd' or whatever and if it is sold the No. of the Ticket left by the Van driver.

Secondly, a similar summary to the 'House' book plus two columns for natural mortality.

Thirdly, census forms which can be used in conjunction with the count.

Fourthly, 'at a glance' graph of the ages of the cull – put an X in the box for each deer shot and the picture will build up.

Fifthly, there is a pad of 'blank' heads. This is useful to record interesting heads seen or shot and can be stuck in the 'House' Book or clipped in the Stalker's Folder.

Deer Management Consultants, Middleton House, Longparish, Andover, Hants.

Census Figures

DATE	WHERE SEEN	MATURE STAGS	YOUNG STAGS	MATURE HINDS	CALVES	YOUNG HINDS	TOTAL MALES	TOTAL FEMALES	GRAND TOTAL	EST. STAG CULL	EST HIND CULL	ACTUAL STAG CULL	ACTUAL HIND CULL	TOTAL CULL

Summary

YEAR	Nos. SHOT															AV. AGE	HUMMEL & MALFORM	Nos. of STAGS BY POINTS													AV. POINTS	TOTAL WEIGHT	AV. WEIGHT	HEAVIEST WEIGHT	No. STAGS FOUND DEAD	No. HINDS FOUND DEAD	REMARKS
	C	1	2	3	4	5	6	7	8	9	10	11	12	13	14	Over			2	3	4	5	6	7	8	9	10	11	12	13	14	Over							
											Nos. of DEER SHOT IN EACH AGE																											
19 STAGS																																						
19 / HINDS																																						
19 STAGS																																						
19 / HINDS																																						
19 STAGS																																						
19 / HINDS																																						
19 STAGS																																						
19 / HINDS																																						
19 STAGS																																						
19 / HINDS																																						
19 STAGS																																						
19 / HINDS																																						
19 STAGS																																						
19 / HINDS																																						
19 STAGS																																						
19 / HINDS																																						
19 STAGS																																						
19 / HINDS																																						

19____

STAG or HIND	No.	DATE	SHOT BY	WHERE SHOT	STALKER	POINTS	AGE	LARDER WEIGHT	VAN WEIGHT	DISPOSAL TO	TICKET No.

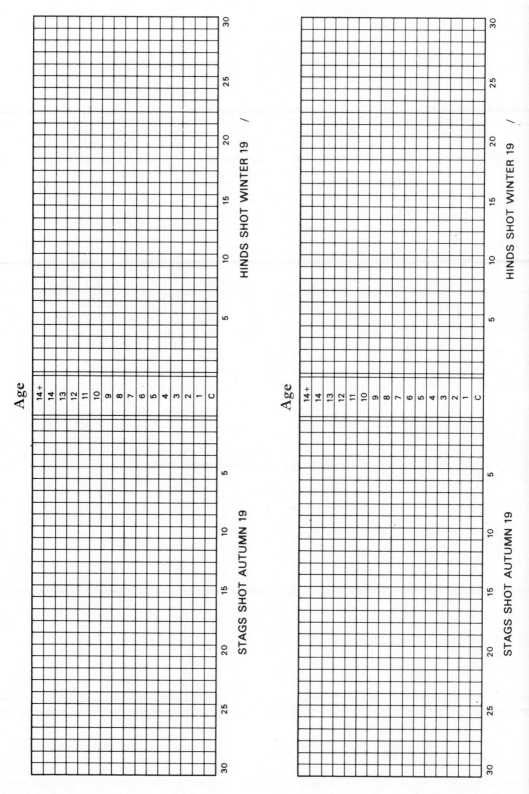

Notes on Using the Roe Management Forms

You will find a folder with the census forms (RM1) and these are for the use of whoever is going to do the count. You will see that the form is divided morning and evening for the five working days of the week. We suggest that the counter enters his count by sticking pins into a map as well as entering his sightings on the form. He will, though, have to adjust at the end of the week for those animals which he has seen more than once, so that the figure under 'total number of roe seen' need not necessarily be the total of the columns above. There is a final total which is the figure he sends into the Office and this figure is entered on RM2. Somebody then does a calculation with our help if you like, and fills in the estimated cull column on RM2, and this figure is also entered on the very last line on RM1 so that whoever is responsible for the beat knows what he is aiming to cull.

The buck cull will start on May 1st as soon as the count is complete. There are two sheets to be filled in as the bucks are shot. One RM3 form should be kept in the 'office' and a further one should be kept by whoever is responsible for the cull. Enter on the left the numerical number 1 for the first one, 2, 3, 4 etc., the date, the weight (this is normally always head on, legs on, completely eviscerated – if the head is cut off before the carcase is sold to the game dealer put this fact under 'Notes'). Disposal could be the name of the game dealer, or 'house'. 'Notes' could contain remarks such as saddle damaged by shot, or anything that may effect the price, or if it is a trophy, how the trophy fee was arrived at. If it was a doe, was she carrying a foetus (twins?).

The other form is the 'game book' record giving the details of the buck shot. With the average type of head it is not of vital interest accurately to record the average length, span and circumference but it is worth taking a little trouble with any head over nine inches as this can be classed as a trophy and the information could be very valuable if the stalking were let to a Continental. The right-hand column on that page is to denote that there is a photograph or sketch of the head, this should be put under the cellophane of the stiff sheets together with the tear-out slip giving the details of the head. (RBC stands for 'round both coronets'. The skull weight must be measured in grammes.) You might like to keep the buck record and photographs in one end of the folder, and the statistical records the other end.

I hope it does not seem over-complicated. There is nothing magical in it, and I imagine they are virtually the same records as you keep for the management of your beef herd or sheep flock – the only difference being that you can't round roe up and send them to market.

R.M.1 Roe Census

BEAT.................................... WEEK...................

		TIME	M.B.	Y.B.	M.D.	Y.D.	TOTAL	NOTES – SKETCHES – PLACE – WIND – WEATHER – P.T.O. if necessary
MON	AM							
	PM							
TUES	AM							
	PM							
WED	AM							
	PM							
THUR	AM							
	PM							
FRI	AM							
	PM							
No. of INDIVIDUAL ROE SEEN								
ESTIMATED No of ROE NOT SEEN								
FINAL TOTAL							FIGURES SENT IN	
SHOOTING PLAN							TARGET FIGURE FOR CULL	

R.M.2

Roe Record

Summary of Season 19 /

BEAT	April Count					Estimated Cull				Actual Cull				No Found Dead	TOTAL		TOTAL
	M.B.	Y.B.	M.D.	Y.D.	TOTAL	M.B.	Y.B.	M.D.	Y.D.	M.B.	Y.B.	M.D.	Y.D.		B.	D.	£p

Roe Buck Records 19 /

No.	Date	Place	Shot By	Pts	Average Length	Span	R.B.C.	Age	Remarks

Roe
Record of Cull

R.M.3   19 /

No	DATE	BEAT	SHOT BY	SEX	AGE	WEIGHT	DISPOSAL	TICKET No	£ p Venison	£ p Trophy	NOTES

ORGANISATIONS CONCERNED WITH DEER

British Deer Farmers Association, Hon. Secretary, Holly Lodge, Spencers Lane, Berkswell, Coventry CV7 7BZ

The British Deer Society, Beale Centre, Lower Basildon, Reading RG8 9NH

Deer Management Consultants, Middleton Estate, Longparish, Andover, Hants

Forestry Commission, 231 Corstorphine Road, Edinburgh EH12 7AT

Game Conservancy, Fordingbridge, Hants SP6 1EF

Mammal Society, c/o Institute of Biology, 41 Queen's Gate, London SW1

National Game Dealers' Association, 1 Belgrove, Tunbridge Wells, Kent TN1 1YW

Red Deer Commission, Knowsley, 82 Fairfield Road, Inverness IV3 5LH

FURTHER READING

ARDREY, R., (1967), *The Territorial Imperative*, Collins. (General background to behaviour.)

BANG and DAHLSTROM, (1974), *Animal Tracks and Signs*, Collins.

BAVARIA, Duke of, (1977), *Über Rehe*, B.L.V., Munich.

BRITISH DEER SOCIETY, (1982), *Field Guide to British Deer*, B.D.S.

BRITISH DEER SOCIETY, (1976), *Deer Control*, B.D.S. (Concerning the setting-up of deer control societies.)

BURTON, M., (1961), *Animal Senses*, Routledge & Kegan Paul.

CHAPLIN, R., (1966), *Reproduction in British Deer*, Passmore Edwards Museum.

CHAPLIN, R., (1977), *Deer*, Blandford. (Biological background to deer natural history.)

CHAPMAN, D. and N., (1975), *The Fallow Deer*, Terence Dalton Ltd. (The only serious work on fallow in English.)

CROWE, S., (1978), *The Landscape of Forests and Woods*, Forestry Commission Booklet 44, H.M.S.O.

DARLING, F. FRASER, (1937), *A Herd of Red Deer*, O.U.P. (A standard reference work.)

EDWARDS, L. and WALLACE, F., (1930), *Hunting and Stalking the Deer*, Longmans Green.

FITTER, R., (1959), *The Ark in our Midst*, Collins. (Introduced species.)

FORESTRY COMMISSION, (1982), *The Fallow Deer*, Forest Record 124, H.M.S.O.

FORESTRY COMMISSION, (1974), *The Roe Deer*, Leaflet No. 99, H.M.S.O.

GATHORNE HARDY A.E., (1900), *Autumns in Argyllshire*, 2nd edition, Longmans Green. (Accounts of moving deer.)

HORWOOD, M.T. and MASTERS, E.H., (1982), *Sika Deer*, British Deer Society

HOLMES, F., (1974), *Following the Roe*, Bartholomew. (An important work on Scottish roe deer.)

KIRCHOFF, (1976), *Dictionary of Hunting*, B.L.V., Munich.

KREBS, H., (1966), *Young or Old?* F.C. Mayer. (A good photo guide.)

LEVER, C., (1977), *Naturalised Animals of the British Isles*, Hutchinson.

LUXMOORE, E., (1980), *Deer Stalking*, David and Charles.

MILLAIS, J.G., (1897), *British Deer and their Horns*, Sotheran.

MITCHELL, STAINES and WELCH, (1977), *Ecology of Red Deer*, I.T.E.

DE NAHLIK, A.J., (1992), *Management of Deer and their Habitat*, Wilson Hunt.

DE NAHLIK, A.J., (1959), *Wild Deer*, Faber & Faber. (A useful translation of continental deer lore.

PEPPER, H., (1978), *Chemical Deterrents*, Forestry Commission Leaflet No. 73, H.M.S.O.

PRIOR, R., (1968), *The Roe Deer of Cranborne Chase*, O.U.P.

PRIOR, R., (1987), *Roe Stalking*, Game Conservancy.

PRIOR, R., (1985), *Modern Roe Stalking*, Tideline Books.

PRIOR, R., (1993), *Deer Watch*, Swan Hill Press.

PUTMAN, R., (1988), *The Natural History of Deer*, Helm.

RED DEER COMMISSION, (1979), *The Next 20 Years*, R.D.C. Inverness. (Conference papers.)

RED DEER COMMISSION, (1981), *Red Deer Management*, H.M.S.O.

ROWE, J.J., (1979), *High Seats for Deer Management*, Forestry Commission Leaflet No. 74, H.M.S.O.

ROWE, J.J., (1976), *Badger Gates*, Forestry Commission Leaflet No. 68, H.M.S.O.

SANDYS-WINSCH, G., (1985), *Gun Law*, 4th edition, Shaw & Sons. (Useful reference book.)

SANDYS-WINSCH, G., (1984), *Animal Law*, 2nd edition, Shaw & Sons. (Useful reference book.)

VON RAESFELD, (1956), *Das Rehwild*, Paul Parey, Hamburg. (The standard German reference book.)

SNAFFLE, the Marquis Iveagh, (1904), *The Roe Deer*, Harwar. (The first work in English on this subject.)

SOPER, E., (1969), *Muntjac*, Longmans Green. (Account of a semi-domesticated community.)

STEELE, R.C. (1972), *Wildlife Conservation in Woodlands*, Forestry Commission Booklet 29, H.M.S.O.

TEGNER, H., (1981), *The Roe Deer*, 2nd edition, Tideline.

TEGNER, H., (1953), *The Buck of Lordenshaw*, Batchworth. (An excellent account of a fictional Northumberland buck.)

TITEUX, G., (1981), *L'Amenagement des Territoires*, Gerfault Club Paris.

VAN DYKE, T.S., (1904), *The Still Hunter*, Macmillan. (North American origin but excellent advice.)

WHITEHEAD, G.K., (1972), *Deer of the World*, Constable. (A general reference book.)

WHITEHEAD, G.K., (1972), *The Wild Goats of Great Britain and Ireland*, David & Charles. (The only work on the subject.)

WHITEHEAD, G.K. *et al.*, (1981), *Game Trophies of the World*, Paul Parey, Hamburg. (Measurement formulae for all species.)

WHITEHEAD, G.K., (1992), *The Whitehead Encyclopedia of Deer*, Swan Hill Press.

WHITEHEAD, G.K., (1980), *Hunting and Stalking Deer in Britain*, Batsford.

WHITEHEAD, G.K., (1982), *Hunting and Stalking Deer throughout the World*, Batsford.

REFERENCES

1. PRIOR, R., (1968), *The Roe Deer of Cranborne Chase*, O.U.P., p. 9.

2. COOPER, A.B. and MUTCH, W.E.S., (1978), 'The Management of Red Deer in Plantations' in E.D. FORD, D.C. MALCOLM and J. ATTERSON (eds.), *The Ecology of Even-aged Plantations*, Div. I, IUFRO, Edinburgh, pp. 453–62.

3. BUBENIK, A., (1960), 'Le Rythme Nycthémeral et le Régime Journalier des Ongulés Sauvages, *Mammalia 24*, pp. 277–85.

4. CADMAN, A., (1966), *Dawn Dusk & Deer*, Country Life, p. 59.

5. BENNETSEN, N.E., (1982), 'Estimation of the Bark Stripping Damage by Sika', *Deer 5*, No. 7, p. 350.

6. SZUKIEL, E., (1981) 'Food Preferences of Deer in Relation to Winter Fodder', *Acta Theriol 26*, pp. 16–28.

7. MITCHELL, STAINES and WELCH, (1977), *Ecology of Red Deer*, I.T.E.

8. TABBUSH, P., (1979), 'Roe Deer Control and Restocking in the Border Forests', *Scottish Forestry 33*, No. 4, pp. 290–4.

9. ROWE, J.J., *Badger Gates*, Forestry Commission Leaflet No. 68, H.M.S.O.

10. PEPPER, H.W., (1992), *Forest Fencing*, Forestry Commission Bulletin 102, H.M.S.O.

11. HAMILTON, W., (pers. com.).

12. LORENZ, K., (1954), *Man Meets Dog*, Methuen, p. 117.

13. TEE, L. and ROE, M., (May 1980), 'Electric and Mesh Fences. A Comparison. *Forestry & British Timber*, p. 25.

14. PEPPER, H.W., ROWE, J.J. and TEE, L.A., (1985), *Individual Tree Protection*, Forestry Commission Leaflet 10, H.M.S.O.

15. PEPPER, H.W., (1978), *Chemical Deterrents*, H.M.S.O.

16. DARLING, F. FRASER, (1951), 'Mammals and Forestry Paper' read at the British Association Sect. Zoology, p. 413.

17. HOFMANN, R.R., (1978), *Wildbiologische Informationen fur den Jager*, Jagd & Hege Verlag, St Gallen.

18. DAVIES, E.S.M., (1981), 'Galloway Deer Control' *Deer 5*, No. 5, p. 228.

19. VAN DYKE, T., (1904), *The Still Hunter*, Macmillan.

20. TITEUX, G., (1981), *L'amenagement des Territoires*, Gerfaut Club, Paris.

21. STEELE, R.C., (1972), *Wildlife Conservation in Woodlands*, H.M.S.O.

22. HARRIMAN, R. and MORRISON, B.R.S., (May 1981), 'Forestry Fisheries and Acid Rain in Scotland, *Scottish Forestry*.

23. MILLS, D.H. (1980), *The Management of Forest Streams*, H.M.S.O.

24. GAME CONSERVANCY, (1981), *Woodlands for Pheasants*.

25. GAME CONSERVANCY, (1980), *Game and Shooting Crops*.

26. VAN DYKE, T., (1904), *The Still Hunter*, Macmillan.

27. BUBENIK, A., (1960), 'Le Rythme Nycthémeral et le Régime Journalier des Ongulés Sauvages', *Mammalia 24*, pp. 277–85.

28. PRIOR, R., (1968), *The Roe Deer of Cranborne Chase*, O.U.P., p. 47.

29. HERMANSSON, N. and BOETHIUS, J. (eds.), (1974), *Algen*, Svenska Jagareforbundet.

30. ROWE, J., (1979), *High Seats for Deer Management*, Forestry Commission Leaflet No. 74, H.M.S.O.

31. *Jaktjournalen*, (January 1982), p. 22.

32. WINDHAM-WRIGHT, M., (1982), 'Trophies for Taxidermy', *Scottish Sporting Gazette*, p. 62.

33. WHITEHEAD, G.K. *et al.*, (1980), *Game Trophies of the World*, Paul Parey.

34. WITCHELL, A., (1981), 'A Deer for All Reasons', *Humberts Review*, p. 25.

35. DE NAHLIK, A.H., (1974), *Deer and Their Management*, David & Charles.

36. TABBUSH, P., (1979), 'Roe Deer Control and Restocking in the Border Forests, *Scottish Forestry 33*, No. 4, pp. 290–4.

37. RED DEER COMMISSION, (1981), *Red Deer Management*, H.M.S.O.

38. COOPER, A.B. and MUTCH, W.E.S., loc. sit.

39. CHAPMAN, D. and N., (1975), *Fallow Deer*, Dalton.

40. LOWE, V.P.W. and GARDINER, A.S., (1976), 'The Red Deer of Furness', *Deer 4*, No. 1, p. 28.

41. HORWOOD, M.T. and MASTERS, E.H., (1981), *Sika Deer*, British Deer Society, p. 7.

42. BENNETSEN, N.E., (1982), 'Estimation of the Bark Stripping Damage done by Sika', *Deer 5*, No. 7, p. 350.

43. HORWOOD, M.T., (1971), 'Sika Deer Research', *Second Progress Report*, N.C.C.

44.   PRIOR, R., (1978), *Roe Deer Management & Stalking*, Game Conservancy.

45.   COOKE, A. and FARRELL, L., (1981), 'The Ecology of Chinese Water Deer on Woodwalton Fen' in B.D.S. Symposium papers *Asiatic Deer*, p. 35.

46.   LAWRENCE, R.P., (4–10 March, 1982), 'Chinese Water Deer' in *Shooting Times*, p. 29.

47.   WHITEHEAD, G.K., (1964), *The Deer of Great Britain & Ireland*, Routledge & Kegan Paul, p. 220.

48.   BATCHELOR, C.L., (1960), 'A Study of the Relations between Roe, Red and Fallow Deer with Special Reference to Drummond Hill, Scotland', *Journal of Animal Ecology* *29*, pp. 375–84.

49.   PATCH, D. and LINES, R., (1981), 'Winter Shelter for Agricultural Stock', *Arboricultural Research*, Note 35/81, Forestry Commission.

50.   POTTER, M.J., (1991), *Tree Shelters*, Forestry Commission Handbook 7, H.M.S.O.

51.   RATCLIFFE, P.R., and MAYLE, B.A., (1992), Roe Deer Biology and Management, Forestry Commission Bulletin 105, H.M.S.O.

Index